NEW DIRECTIONS FOR CHILD DEVELOPMENT

William Damon, *Brown University*
EDITOR-IN-CHIEF

The Development of Political Understanding: A New Perspective

Helen Haste
University of Bath, England

Judith Torney-Purta
University of Maryland

EDITORS

D1522558

Number 56, Summer 1992

JOSSEY-BASS PUBLISHERS
San Francisco

THE DEVELOPMENT OF POLITICAL UNDERSTANDING: A NEW PERSPECTIVE
Helen Haste, Judith Torney-Purta (eds.)
New Directions for Child Development, no. 56
William Damon, Editor-in-Chief

Microfilm copies of issues and articles are available in 16mm and 35mm,
as well as microfiche in 105mm, through University Microfilms Inc., 300
North Zeeb Road, Ann Arbor, Michigan 48106.

LC 85-644581   ISSN 0195-2269   ISBN 1-55542-752-9

NEW DIRECTIONS FOR CHILD DEVELOPMENT is part of The Jossey-Bass
Education Series and is published quarterly by Jossey-Bass Inc., Publish-
ers (publication number USPS 494-090). Second-class postage paid at
San Francisco, California, and at additional mailing offices. POSTMASTER:
Send address changes to Jossey-Bass Inc., Publishers, 350 Sansome Street,
San Francisco, California 94104.

EDITORIAL CORRESPONDENCE should be sent to the Editor-in-Chief,
William Damon, Department of Education, Box 1938, Brown University,
Providence, Rhode Island 02912.

Cover photograph by Wernher Krutein/PHOTOVAULT © 1990.

CONTENTS

INTRODUCTION

This volume, *The Development of Political Understanding: A New Perspective,* brings together current thinking on young people and politics. The book moves away from traditional questions about party affiliation and attitudes, many of which appear peripheral even to many adults. It concentrates instead on the way political, economic, social, and moral issues of the public world are understood and interwoven with everyday private thinking. The argument is that we can only understand the specific and narrow forms of political beliefs that are reflected in voting and other explicitly political actions if we understand how the elements of political thought become part of everyday social understanding.

The common theoretical framework of these chapters derives from studies of cognitive developmental psychology and of social cognition. People are active agents in the construction of their own meaning systems, and so the cognitive structures or schemata that they bring to understanding a situation and the scenarios that they envision are of vital importance. But, in contrast with traditional cognitive developmental models, these chapters emphasize the role of culture, of negotiation, and of social representations. The individual's process of actively making sense of the social world occurs within a context and set of social constructions of that world. We can understand individual cognition only by seeing how it develops in interaction with others, facilitated or limited by the constructions of reality available to the growing person in society.

How the boundaries have been set around what is considered political has depended very much on the concerns and theoretical perspective of the researcher. Those who conceptualize political development as socialization see the young person molded by social forces into a political orientation. The implied question is how a society is reproduced from one generation to the next. Also this view implies a normative set of behavior associated with citizenship. A socialization model looks for the antecedent conditions such as social class or direct inculcation of parental beliefs. The outcome criteria are frequently attitudes or attitude-related behaviors such as voting, however infrequent in occurrence. The methodology of the political socialization approach necessarily involves large-scale surveys to afford a representative picture within which group differences can be seen.

In contrast, a focus on the development of political awareness shifts the emphasis to the individual's construction of the political world. The question is, how does he or she enter into increased understanding of

Editorial support for this book was provided by the Graduate Research Board, University of Maryland, College Park, through a semester award.

concepts and build a complex organization of beliefs and values? The implication is that the individual is active in this process, constructing private meanings for public concepts. Social class, ethnic group, and agents of education may limit or facilitate the individual's construction but they do not determine its outcome. For example, the young person may assimilate some communications from the teacher or parent while ignoring or rejecting others. The substantive questions of political development tend to be less about party affiliation and more about a wider conception of the political world, including one's understanding of society and power. What constitutes political participation is also broadly defined. The methodology of this approach to political development is designed to document processes of individual thought and of discourse. It therefore includes interviews as well as surveys.

These two theoretical approaches to the political domain reflect common divisions within psychology. They may be contrasted with a third approach that has been used to account for political attitudes in terms of personality dynamics such as authoritarianism. Although this approach has been criticized, there is some revival of interest in its fundamental tenets. It is mentioned here because it is a way of cutting across the left-right continuum so common in political attitude research. According to this approach, the conditions of individual development pertinent to affect, predisposition toward openness and flexibility, and tolerance of ambiguity are central to the development of political attitudes. These personality models have in common with developmental models the assumption that an individual is attracted to a particular belief system, rather than simply amenable to its imposition by external forces.

Much research has arisen out of these three theoretical approaches. However, many studies have also originated in response to public events. Psychologists have never been particularly tuned into a historical perspective. Thus, when watershed events occur or social movements arise, psychologists are seldom in the forefront. With respect to both the civil rights movement and the women's movement, it took several years before many psychologists mounted research or considered the philosophical, methodological, and theoretical implications of these events. Feminist consciousness was relatively well established before most psychologists challenged the frequent use of gender role stereotypes as the basis for classifications of personal adjustment, for example. Yet, within about a decade there was a great deal of research based on changed gender role concepts. Similarly, it took the student revolution of the 1960s to challenge the bland prevailing view of citizenship and political participation. Researchers gradually began to envision unconventional political participation (meaning participation in boycotts or demonstrations) as well as conventional participation (voting or writing letters to the newspaper) as part of the repertoire available to the average citizen and not just to the university student.

A practical concern that has driven research is the need for educational programs to prepare young people to undertake adult citizen roles. Sigel and Hoskin (1981, p. 41), who did one of the most recent large-scale studies of political socialization, defined participation in a way compatible with what we are considering here: "Political involvement to us involves everything and anything which will affect the quality and character of our public lives—so long as it could potentially come under the aegis of government." This kind of definition has very different implications for research on political development and citizenship education than does a definition focused mainly on political party identification or voting behavior.

In a society as self-conscious about its democracy as the United States, citizenship means widespread active participation, and training for citizenship is taken very seriously. However, education for citizenship has focused much more on the conventional than on the unconventional forms of political activity and on consensual rather than controversial issues. In Britain, however, civic education has largely been confined, at least until the recent introduction of a national curriculum, to peripheral aspects of "general studies" (Torney-Purta, 1984). In the mainstream view of citizenship common to both countries, political activity means activity designed to influence policy, to make political leaders aware of the views at the grass roots, and to ensure a system that maintains accountability and communication.

The historical backgrounds of these two countries reveal a lack of commonality in the views of citizenship and political awareness as well. The exercise of one's democratic rights is deemed to be both the birthright and the obligation of Americans; it is conceived as consensually based activity and was not, at least until the 1960s, generally regarded as involving challenge to the power or legitimacy of social institutions. Since that decade, a distinction has been made between conventional political activity in this consensual mode and unconventional political activity that calls into question, changes, or even undermines the political system.

The history of European democracies has been more of a struggle between power groups—the weaker, poorer, and less powerful against the strong and entrenched. Conventional political activity is important, as is consensual politics, but the folk memories of necessary struggle and conflicting group interests remain and often surface in political rhetoric. American democracy is frequently portrayed as the creation of people who fled the oppression of European groups to set up a self-consciously consensual system. In contrast, European political systems, while equally democratic in the sense of the accountability of political leaders and open elections, show more overt awareness that major social identity factors such as class and economic status can handicap the power of the citizen both individually and in groups. For our purposes, it is important to note that for many decades socially constructed schemata that underlie an understanding of conflict and that provide bases for ideologies such as socialism have been part of public discourse in most Western European countries but have had no real counterpart in the United States.

In the 1960s in the United States, confrontational forms of participation did emerge in some groups in response to their assumption that those in power were resisting change, favoring small elite groups, and unwilling to cede power. There was a new awareness of the nature of political power and of new forms of participation, many of which involved both personal inconvenience and risk to job or future plans. This new awareness created an image of the political actor quite different from that of the good adult citizen who votes regularly, writes letters to the newspaper, and volunteers in community betterment projects. The availability of these new schemata for power and scenarios of participation in the political culture has been only partially reflected in the day-to-day citizenship education that takes place in American schools, however.

In the late 1960s, research on moral development and on the moral dimensions of political action and thought introduced a new dimension. Citizens usually perform the duty of voting or of community volunteering without defining the situation in terms of principled moral choice. In contrast, the process of becoming involved in protests often entails willingness to take substantial risks in the belief that one's cause is just. Thus, the issue of political participation becomes an issue of moral choice. The research relating Kohlberg's stages of moral reasoning to political activism, to interpretation of political issues, and to political beliefs provided one way of understanding individuals who choose unconventional political activity (Weinreich-Haste, 1986). It also implied that a developmental model might be appropriate; if political action and political beliefs are related to stage of moral development, one might expect to find powerful developmental processes in the realm of political awareness.

Even in the mid-1960s and quite separate from youth protest, a developmental model of political socialization had been used in the work of Hess and Torney (1967) and Adelson and O'Neil (1966). Hess and Torney conducted a large-scale survey of elementary school students, but age trends were interpreted using a cognitive developmental model. Their exploratory interview data illustrated the processes by which primary school children constructed political ideas and incorporated new information. Adelson and O'Neil (1966) used a neo-Piagetian framework to look at the development of a number of key ideas: community, law, and individual rights. They found marked developmental change among adolescents: a movement toward greater abstraction and generalization, and a shift from authoritarian to more democratic methods of social control. Many other studies subsequently confirmed an increasing understanding of government and society as abstract collective entities to which the individual is bound in a kind of social contract.

One political issue in particular sparked considerable research and had important theoretical implications as well. In the early 1980s, a number of surveys documented that young people, including quite small children, were very concerned about the threat of nuclear war. This finding was important because most previous studies had found political issues to be separate from personal concerns. People might feel a community obligation or a loyalty to political party, but these types of social commitments hardly competed with personal concerns about relationships, career, or school. Several studies showed that fear of nuclear war was nearly as prevalent as fears such as losing one's parents or failing in school.

A consequence of this overlap between a political issue and a personal concern seemed to be increased awareness of other public issues, and, in many cases, greater participation in action to influence public opinion or government officials. Writers spoke of empowerment both as a constructive response to fear and as an element that increased political attentiveness in general. The nuclear issue touched people personally and facilitated a bridging of the gap between public and private concerns. Previously, this bridging happened primarily for blacks involved in the civil rights movement or females involved in women's rights activities. In other words, political issues of great personal consequence such as nuclear war seemed to touch people who were not otherwise politicized.

Currently, the connection of political issues and personal concerns can be seen in the surge of interest in environmental issues. The importance of the "green movement" does not lie primarily in the formation of political parties but rather in the fact that people of all ages can be personally and practically involved and see the effects of a lack of concern for the environment. Environmental issues seem to have the power to politicize, to make people aware of connections between the public and the private, and to motivate action. These issues, including their political dimensions, contrast with many others on the public agenda in that they are perceived as appropriate to discuss with children. In Britain, the influential television program "Blue Peter" has produced a book that contains both practical advice about what the individual child can do to improve environmental conditions and a discussion of the broader social and political issues of environmentalism. It has been designed to empower children of about eight years old by giving them a sense of personal efficacy, not only to clean up their neighborhoods but to be watchful of what governments do about the environment. A similar program has been produced in the United States as part of the "Mr. Rogers's Neighborhood" series on public television, and these issues are frequently also discussed on "Sesame Street" (as well as in many elementary school science and social studies curricula).

We have discussed the different theoretical models in psychology that have been employed to understand the emergence of political ideas. We have also attempted to show how the development of this understanding embraces many aspects of the public and private domains and of their interrelationship. Our approach in general does not completely ignore party affiliation or voting but recognizes that the beliefs and values that ultimately lead to a particular vote are grounded in the individual's system for making sense of the way in which social and political institutions influence personal relationships as well as material and moral well-being. Although the casting of ballots is not an everyday occurrence, beliefs about what causes unemployment and whether there should be laws to penalize companies that pollute the environment touch aspects of everyday life and reflect the cognitive structures that people have developed to understand their lives.

The Chapters in This Volume

The focus of this volume is political understanding. The authors deal very little with socialization models of the influence of independent variables on attitudes or with psychodynamic forces that may influence political beliefs. But neither are the contributors to this volume mainstream cognitive developmental psychologists applying models of understanding developed in the domain of the physical world to the domain of public issues. Nor are they seeking stages of political understanding that parallel stages of moral development. The strength of the developmental model used here is the recognition of the enormous range of competencies and systems of meaning that people bring to the political domain and the focus on the role of the individual in making sense of information and experience, that is, how he or she constructs a private concept or understanding of a public issue. In this individual construction of social and political ideas there is growth and the development of new cognitive functions during childhood and adolescence.

A major limitation of the traditional developmental approach is that it is too focused on what happens inside individuals' heads and not sufficiently tuned to the social and historical context of everyday life. It is within this context that the germs of political ideas become available to the growing individual. The traditional approach also neglects the social processes that facilitate or inhibit particular constructions.

The contributors here share the perspective that people make sense of their world and the repertoire of political concepts that it offers through negotiation and in dialogue with others. In making sense of the world, they draw upon and may be limited by the political schemata within the wider culture that are the common social currency of groups within which the individual moves. The salience of these schemata is contingent on two things: First, are they useful? Utility depends on both their perceived relevance to contemporary life and factors such as their identification with particular ideological positions. Second, are they comprehensible to the individual? This is a matter of the complexity of the ideas and their consistency with underlying assumptions. For example, a schema that relates political crises to a calculation of individual and group interests is too complex for most individuals to understand, and a schema that relates such crises to divine punishment for sin is incompatible with the prevailing, underlying assumptions about political life found in the United States and Britain.

Some of the contributors to this volume emphasize the availability of political schemata and scenarios; others emphasize the cognitive developmental process and the growth of a capacity to understand complex political arguments. But, overall, their approach, in contrast to conventional attitude research, is to look at the frameworks of meaning that people bring to the task of making sense of the world. Each framework is based on a "theory" about how things work in the social and political world at both the institutional and the personal levels. Theory may sound like too grand a term for adolescents' political views, but it is used here in much the same way that Carey (1985) describes the young child's theories as conceptual networks about biological organisms and physical characteristics of objects. The term encompasses the idea that young people have knowledge, put it together in ways that seem meaningful, and use it to interpret and formulate explanations of what happens in the world. Social cognition researchers have increasingly demonstrated that beneath common attitudes lie theorylike preferences for particular explanations of personal and institutional functioning. Studies of young people are particularly important because in the process of development there is an increasingly complex appreciation of the relevant social and political phenomena to be accounted for. The theories and schemata that can be used to interpret these political phenomena and the scenarios of what happens in politics are also elaborated.

Three themes run throughout this volume, each arising from the presupposition that the individual is an agent in constructing meaning, but that this construction takes place within a social, cultural, and historical context. The first theme is that to understand political development, we must look at the cognitive structures or schemata that individual young people hold, the scenarios of action that they envision, and the "lay theories" that they draw upon to account for experience. In one way or another, all of the chapters here describe development as increasing complexity and differentiation in these schemata of the political and social world.

In Chapter One, Judith Torney-Purta explores how American adolescents use schemata and representations to understand discourse, to organize memory for ideas about the political system, to comprehend problems, and to provide cognitive structures to which attitudes can be attached. The progression in development is toward more elaborated schemata that include a clearer grasp of how national and international political systems operate. She lays out a continuum of adolescents' expertise, composed of the categories pre-novice, novice, and post-novice and related to increasingly elaborated content of their political schemata. Interviews with adult experts document the existence of two additional points on the continuum—pre-expert and expert—which are distinguished by the approach to constructing problems before proposing solutions. Attitudes, for example, toward apartheid, are seen as attached to these individually constructed cognitive representations rather than as free-floating valences toward objectively defined attitude objects.

Helen Haste, in Chapter Two, also deals with political schemata and adds the notion of "lay social theory." She illustrates the common schemata found across the widely divergent areas of adolescents' reasoning in regard to personal, interpersonal, and sociopolitical issues. She also documents different styles of thinking or ways of organizing schemata that are consistent over these subdomains. Her four case studies of British young people show them drawing on different schemata and envisioning different scenarios, differences that can be interpreted in the light of their respective social backgrounds and contexts. In addition, she relates stage of moral reasoning to the complexity of the scenarios and schemata drawn upon.

The ways in which individuals give specific private meanings to generalized public concepts and the ways in which they employ different scenarios for understanding the world are also illustrated by Patricia G. Avery, in Chapter Three. In moving beyond the usual characterization of political tolerance as a free-floating belief about what some generalized unpopular group should be allowed to do in the public forum, she shows that it is important to ask the individual about the particular group in American society that he or she finds most distasteful for its beliefs. Willingness to tolerate political activity by that particular group reflects the individual's construction, not merely the society's representation, of the political scene. Further, Avery demonstrates the importance of scenarios of actions that the individual associates with the practice of free speech. Asked about the consequences of allowing a rally by Nazis or by gay rights activists, tolerant students consider possible negative consequences such as confrontation but weigh these against the right to free assembly in the context of a differentiated view of the dissenting group. Intolerant students, in contrast, foresee an almost inevitably violent scenario of confrontation in the context of a relatively undifferentiated negative view of the group.

In Chapter Four, Fayneese Miller makes the point that the individual's way of thinking about political issues and their relevance to the self is an important and often ignored aspect of political activity and involvement. She explores the way in which American adolescents interpret public issues to make them personally salient to their instrumental actions, a framework that often includes a scenario of perceived consequences. She contrasts issues constructed in this way with issues involving a socialized symbolic belief in an abstract value (such as responsibility for others) lacking a connection to consequences for the individual's personal well-being. She presents data that show the complexity of some adolescents' reasoning in weighing the consequences of issues for self and society.

The second of our themes, the relationship between development of understanding and social context, is addressed by Helen Haste but is taken up much more extensively by Nicholas Emler, in Chapter Five. He explores the developing understanding of formal authority among Scottish and French children and concludes that the school is a forum in which both the enactment of authority relations and its attendant discourse among teacher and pupils supply an indispensable public context for private development of schemata and scenarios. Emler's chapter also reflects the third theme of the volume, the relationship between certain unique aspects of a given social context and the way in which individuals develop and use representations. Emler describes the socially constructed representations of bureaucracy and authority that circulate in his respondents' communities, giving particular attention to the individual's consciousness and developing complexity of these representations.

Martín Sánchez Jankowski, in Chapter Six, deals even more explicitly with the extent to which different cultural contexts provide the raw material for the different meaning systems of individuals. He looks at the way in which Chicano adolescents (followed in a longitudinal study into young adulthood) make sense of their social position and formulate a political response to it in three different city environments. His interviews show that the ways in which parents and siblings present the realities of political life and the scenarios of consequences for political action reflect the social order of the particular city and the social class position of the family. For example, he contrasts San Antonio, Texas, where parents fear reprisals from the Anglo community for activism, with the more pluralistic world of Los Angeles, where schemata and scenarios for political action are less threatening to the individual.

Finally, in Chapter Seven, Judith Van Hoorn and Paula J. LeVeck rely on Bronfenbrenner's (1979) model of social-ecological systems to describe the social context of adolescents who became young adults in the United States during the 1980s. The authors report changes in individuals' beliefs about nuclear war and focus on three case studies that, over time, illustrate different ways of constructing personal responsibility and commitment related to the microsystem, mesosystem, exosystem, and macrosystem. These constructions reflect different and continuously more complex schemata linking the individual to the social and political world, as well as different agendas for involvement in it.

All of the chapters help us to understand in a new way the complexities of individual constructions of political understanding in a social context by challenging the undifferentiated view that agents of socialization transmit political attitudes and values about participation to passive young people. In many respects, political understanding is an ideal area in which to explore individual and social construction because it presents the private and public worlds in such clear juxtaposition. We hope that this new framework will stimulate more research in the field of political socialization, a field that we reconceptualize here as the study of expansion and differentiation in individuals' private understanding of politics in ways that make public issues meaningful and even compelling.

Helen Haste
Judith Torney-Purta
Editors

References

Adelson, J., and O'Neil, R. "The Growth of Political Ideas in Adolescence: The Sense of Community." *Journal of Personality and Social Psychology,* 1966, *4,* 295–306.
Bronfenbrenner, U. *The Ecology of Human Development: Experiments by Nature and Design.* Cambridge, Mass.: Harvard University Press, 1979.
Carey, S. *Conceptual Change in Childhood.* Cambridge, Mass.: MIT Press, 1985.
Hess, R. D., and Torney, J. V. *The Development of Political Attitudes in Children.* Hawthorne, N.Y.: Aldine, 1967.
Sigel, R., and Hoskin, M. *The Political Involvement of Adolescents.* New Brunswick, N.J.: Rutgers University Press, 1981.
Torney-Purta, J. "Political Socialization and Policy: The U.S. in a Cross-National Context." In H. Stevenson and A. Siegel (eds.), *Child Development Research and Social Policy.* Vol. 1. Chicago: University of Chicago Press, 1984.
Weinreich-Haste, H. "Kohlberg and Politics: A Positive View." In S. Modgil and C. Modgil (eds.), *Kohlberg: Consensus and Controversy.* Lewes, England: Falmer Press, 1986.

HELEN HASTE is senior lecturer in psychology, University of Bath, England. Her research interests include gender and culture, as well as the development of moral, political, and social reasoning among adolescents and young adults.

JUDITH TORNEY-PURTA is professor of human development and affiliate professor of psychology at the University of Maryland, College Park. Her research interests include cross-national research on developmental and educational processes, as well as the application of conceptualizations and methods from cognitive psychology to the study of political socialization.

Socialization is viewed as a process of increasing expertise in the solving of political problems among U.S. adolescents.

Cognitive Representations of the Political System in Adolescents: The Continuum from Pre-Novice to Expert

Judith Torney-Purta

The decline of interest in political socialization research during the past two decades has been widely noted. This chapter argues for a reconceptualization of this field in psychological terms as the study of the development of political cognition, understanding, and expertise. Two phenomena must be accounted for in this approach. First, one must explain the gap between the public's or socialization agents' representations of the functioning of the polity or the international system and the individual adolescent's privately constructed representation of that functioning. When this gap has been noted by survey researchers (Jennings and Niemi, 1981), it has been interpreted as a product of conflict between generations. Interpreted in a cognitive framework, the gap is attributed to the process that begins when young people are exposed to political and social issues in their everyday lives and then use their prior knowledge and attitudes as a basis for constructing representations or understandings of these issues that are meaningful to them. These personal constructions may or may not correspond to the messages that schools or parents have attempted to transmit.

Second, one must explain change over the period from childhood to

Support from the Graduate Research Board at the University of Maryland is gratefully acknowledged.

11

adulthood in representations of politics. Some political socialization researchers have posited stages of political development. Since there is concrete thinking in young children and more abstract thinking in older children, they have concluded that Piagetian stages exist in political thinking in much the same form that they exist in thinking about physical objects (Moore, Lare, and Wagner, 1985). This conclusion ignores the fact that young people acquire information about the political world largely through the oral or written discourse of adults (in person, in textbooks or newspapers, or on television). This discourse-mediated process of contacting the political world contrasts so much with the direct process of observing the effect of actions on the physical world that political socialization seems to require a model of the construction of knowledge specific to this domain rather than an extension of Piaget's stages (Torney-Purta, 1990b). Cognitive and social psychologists who have studied how novices and experts deal with social and political problems (Voss, Tyler, and Yengo, 1983; Fiske, Lau, and Smith, 1990) provide a more useful way of conceptualizing how young people differ from adults in understanding the political domain. Adolescents can be thought of as novices, while adults are at more advanced points along a continuum of expertise.

In summary, the construction by individuals of representations of the social world and associated social identities is neither a totally objective transmission nor a completely subjective process. It is rather an intersubjective process of communication, conflict, construction, and negotiation, both between children and adults and between children and their peers (Duveen and Lloyd, 1990). Everyday political thinking takes place when the adolescent reads a social studies text about the problems of large cities or a newspaper article about a summit conference or participates in a discussion in a classroom or around the dining room table at home. When faced with a political problem to solve or a decision to make, such as whether to participate in a demonstration against apartheid or whether to volunteer for a community recycling project, a cognitive representation of the social and political world is called upon. And although it is important to examine the construction of these representations as a developmental process, there is no necessary reason to believe that it is characterized by clearly bounded stages of thinking generalized from the domain of physical knowledge. The process might be more fruitfully described as gradual acquisition of political expertise.

A Political Socialization Framework Based on Cognitive Psychology

A framework for understanding the content and structure of a young person's cognitive representations of politics should meet several criteria: First, it should be appropriate to political situations that usually lack clear structure and political problems that lack agreed-upon solutions; second, it should take account of the role of discourse and dialogue about social representations; and, third, it should integrate attitudes with cognition. Although the framework should provide an account of the individual's construction over time of a system of representations, it need not have clearly delimited stages of development. It may instead make distinctions about political maturity along the continuum of novice to expert, a continuum that can be applied across the life span. Recent approaches in cognitive psychology and information processing provide a promising starting point for this kind of conceptual framework.

In this framework, meaningful processing of information entails the relating of information to existing cognitive structures, commonly called *representations* or *schemata*. Schemata are *hypothesized* mental structures that help to account for a variety of research findings, for example, differences in the efficiency of various learning modes. These schemata *organize information* that the individual already possesses on a given topic, for example, political parties or the issue of global warming.

Rumelhart (1980) has described several functions of schemata in cognition. Although his theorizing has subsequently moved in a different direction, each of the functions that he described can be related specifically to political socialization. First, schemata serve a function in the understanding of oral or written discourse. The way that an individual understands a reading or a discussion of politics is related to the existing schemata that are activated in response to it. Graber (1988) has described the way in which schemata mediate adults' understanding of discourse in the form of political news. McKeown and Beck (1990) concluded that many elementary students are unlikely to understand much of the written discourse in social studies textbooks. Many fifth graders have, for example, inaccurate schemata associated with the phrase "taxation without representation." They interpret the term *representation* to mean group solidarity in favor of something, as occurred, for example, during the Boston Tea Party, and they interpret text material on the basis of this cognitive structure. Research on political socialization has dealt with participation in discourse or discussion as a way of influencing political views, but there is little research on the ways in which existing cognitive representations shape a young person's reception of new information orally or in writing.

Second, schemata serve a function in learning and recall of new information. A piece of new information may be added to a slot in an existing mental structure through accretion; it may be added but may slightly change or tune the structure or it may be in conflict with the existing structure and cause restructuring. If instruction helps a student develop elaborated schemata, the retrieval of information is facilitated.

Research on socialization has considered this second function of schemata. Berti and Bombi (1988) note that young children possess separate and unconnected schemata for buying and selling and for the production of goods and so have difficulty in learning about the economic system. Hallden (1986) argues that pupils' historical schemata are focused on individuals' personal motivations as the causes of events. Their schemata for an institution are coincident with the individual persons in it. These cognitive representations hamper the storage and retrieval of information presented in school.

Third, schemata serve a function in problem solving. Schemata that store a set of procedures to solve a particular type of problem are involved in the formulation of a cognitive representation of a problem. They are especially important in knowledge-rich domains such as politics. Cognitive processes in adults' problem solving have been studied in relation to topics in economics and politics. Voss, Tyler, and Yengo (1983) developed methods for comparing the processes that novices and experts used to solve social science problems such as the following: "Assume you are the head of the Soviet Ministry of Agriculture, and crop productivity has been low. You have the responsibility of increasing crop productivity. How would you go about doing this? Just think aloud and say whatever comes to mind about how you would solve this problem." In analyzing these think-aloud protocols, Voss, Tyler, and Yengo charted the sequence of different elements of the argument (for example, stating a subproblem and evaluating a solution). They found that professors specializing in Soviet affairs (experts) spent much more time defining a problem and mentioned more constraints on proposed solutions than did the undergraduate respondents (novices).

There is a fourth function of schemata as well. Social psychologists have proposed that attitudes are bipolar or unipolar schemata that influence the storage and recall of information (Pratkanis, 1989), and that the way an individual responds to an attitude survey item can be conceptualized as recall of a cognitive representation of the situation described in the item (Tourangeau, 1987). A recent review of research on intergroup relations dealt primarily with the schemata of ethnic groups used by individuals to encode and retrieve information (Messick and Mackie, 1989). Attitudes toward outgroups were discussed as affect bound to these cognitive representations and not as phenomena that could be measured independently.

In this chapter, I argue for the application of this framework of schemata or cognitive representations to the study of political socialization, defining it as a process by which public knowledge about political institutions and processes and associated attitudes are given private meanings by individuals who internalize or encode the material in their cognitive structures. In other words, representations of knowledge about politics presented in society are received by the young person as he or she listens or reads and are then given meaning in terms of existing cognitive structures. What is actually contained in an individual's cognitive structures, however, may differ in substantial ways from what agents of socialization have attempted to impart and imagine to exist in socializees. Structures containing prior social and political knowledge may be inadequate to assimilate the new knowledge, the individual may process the discourse that contains the information in a nonmeaningful way, or the individual's attitudes may create resistance to certain information. When problems or decisions regarding politics arise in everyday life, they are solved by means of relevant problem-solving schemata.

Studies comparing novices with experts have been a mainstay of research on cognitive structures. This research has special relevance for the schemata model. Most of the research has been conducted on problems in chess, medical diagnosis, and physics. Experts access problem schemata from memory and fit the problems that they are asked to solve into these representations. Key words in the problem may trigger schemata for novices that are different from those triggered for experts. A few hours of instruction provided to adult novices often improve their ability to access more adequate schemata, but this instruction does not entirely make up the differences observed between novices and experts. Thus, the shift from novice to expert is similar to a developmental process in that experience must be assimilated over a relatively long period of time.

Chi, Hutchinson, and Robin (1989) compared seven-year-old novices and experts on the topic of dinosaurs. There were differences between the two groups in the coherence and integration of knowledge but not in the number of discrete bits of knowledge. When given a picture of either a familiar or an unfamiliar dinosaur, expert children were more likely to comment on implicit attributes not pictured (for example, where the dinosaur might live) because knowledge in the dinosaur schema was accessed in response to the image of one exemplar. The researchers concluded that "when experts activate a dinosaur concept node (part of a schema) several other related attributes (implicit knowledge) and concepts also get activated with high strength" (Chi, Hutchinson, and Robin, 1989, p. 38).

Research on political or social knowledge comparing novices and experts is still relatively limited and often has methodological shortcomings. Expertise is often defined with a short multiple-choice test on political knowledge (Fiske, Lau, and Smith, 1990). Or simple behavioral criteria are used; for example, McGraw and Pinney (1990) compared college undergraduates who had filled out a federal income tax return ("experts") with those ("novices") who had not. Research has not yet been conducted on adolescent political socialization as a process of attaining expertise in the form of more complex cognitive structures, more elaborated comprehension of political discourse, and more complex problem-solving strategies.

In studies of political and social expertise, the standard method is to compare only two groups, one relatively more expert than the other, rather than multiple positions on a continuum of expertise. There are only a few studies that deal with more than two groups, the third usually being a group of "post-novices." As a departure from this standard research design, let us suppose the following continuum in the development of political understanding: At the first level are pre-novices, who lack knowledge of the most basic political structures and beliefs; at the second level and the third level are novices and post-novices, who have accessible and knowledge-rich cognitive representations or schemata of politics that are partially differentiated and include some connections; at the fourth level are pre-experts, who not only have a wide range of representations of political actors and actions but also see them with many connections and with more differentiations and complexities than novices; finally, at the fifth level are true experts, who in addition to complex cognitive and attitudinal schemata also have well-developed strategies for defining and solving political problems.

Let us speculate about different age groups on this continuum. Most adolescents would be political pre-novices and novices. These two categories, together with post-novices, probably contain most adult citizens, who have more than basic schemata of politics but seldom practice the problem-solving strategies of the political experts. Utilizing methods derived from cognitive psychology, including this continuum from political pre-novice to political expert, I will now present a particular application of the schemata model in research on political socialization.

Adolescents' Political Representations and Think-Aloud Problem Solving

The research site at which this model was developed is a computer-assisted foreign policy simulation (Project ICONS) that is part of the Maryland Summer Center for International Studies. During each two-week session, twelve- to seventeen-year-olds from Maryland are divided into teams representing diplomats from six nations, such as Brazil, France, and so on. Participants engage in negotiation, during which the teams send messages using a computer-conferencing link. All within-team communication takes place face to face; all between-team communication takes place over the computer network. Heated debate takes place within teams about the wording of these messages. This cognitive conflict among peers is a potent stimulus to restructure social and political schemata (Torney-Purta, 1989). For the study described here, thirty adolescents, fourteen to seventeen years of age, were interviewed before and after their participation in this simulation.

Subjects responded to the following problems in interviews, which were taped and transcribed:

Finance Minister's Debt Problem: Imagine you are the finance minister of a developing country. The interest payment on your debt to banks in developed countries is due, but there is not enough money in your treasury to pay it. What actions would you take to solve this problem? What would you do? What would you ask others to do? Just think aloud and tell me whatever comes to your mind about what you would do to solve this problem if you were the finance minister.

Diplomat's Apartheid Problem: Imagine you are a diplomat. You hear that the government of a neighboring country, let's call it Country C, is planning a system of laws very much like apartheid that would apply to a group of immigrants who are of a different race from the others who live in Country C. Your country is very much against apartheid. What actions would you take? Just think aloud.

Mayor's Toxic Waste Problem: Imagine you are the mayor of a small town. You have been informed that a toxic waste dump containing chemicals from a local company has been found under a school. There is evidence that the students attending this school have a higher than normal rate of cancer. The cost of the cleanup is expected to be so high that the company will go out of business and many jobs will be lost. As the mayor, what actions could you take? Just think aloud.

After the interviewee stops volunteering solutions, the interviewer asks whether there are any problems with the solutions given, whether there are any reasons that they would not work, to probe for perceived constraints.

The second source of data was fifteen students, age fifteen to eighteen, who were participating in an educational program in Washington, D.C. They were interviewed about five problems, one of which was the mayor's toxic waste problem cited above. The third source of data was a group of eight "experts," Coast Guard officials who agreed to be interviewed in their offices by a younger colleague and group leaders from the Maryland Summer Center for International Studies.

A major source of methods for analyzing these sets of interview data was research on logical problem solving and schemata. Hayes and Simon (see Hayes, 1981) studied the process by which an individual encodes written instructions for a complex logical problem, coding the "actors" and "legal" ways for them to operate. There are considerable similarities between their discussion of actors, actions, and constraints on actions in solving logical problems and the way in which specialists in international relations discuss political actors (for example, leaders or international organizations) and actions in which they can engage (for example, negotiation or declaration of war).

Each interview transcript was read and a graphic model of the schemata of the political or economic system implied in the respondent's answer was drawn. The elements of these political-economic schemata included *actors* who might be approached by the finance minister, diplomat, or mayor (for example, banks, other countries opposing apartheid, state environmental protection officials, respectively), *actions* that these actors might be asked to undertake (for example, refinancing the loan, joining an embargo on trade with South Africa, providing funds to clean up the toxic waste, respectively), and *constraints on actions* (for example, banks or countries might not agree or the state might not have funds for cleanup).

These graphic models are similar to semantic network maps. The models are also similar to those used by Voss, Tyler, and Yengo (1983) in that they are drawn from transcripts of think-aloud-solving of social science problems and include constraints; they are different, however, in that these schema-maps deal with the content of schemata (for example, which actors and actions are mentioned and therefore appear to be part of the individual's cognitive representation of the political system) rather than with the sequence of the solution.

As examples, graphic schema-maps for two individuals are presented in Figures 1.1–1.4 for the apartheid problem. (The method is the same for the finance minister's debt problem; see Torney-Purta, 1990a.) The basic elements of the maps, represented by triangles, are the actors mentioned who might be approached by the diplomat in order to solve the problem.

Figure 1.1. Schema Map of Respondent's Presession Answer to the Apartheid Problem, Student in French Diplomat Role

Figure 1.2. Schema Map of Respondent's Postsession Answer to the Apartheid Problem, Student in French Diplomat Role

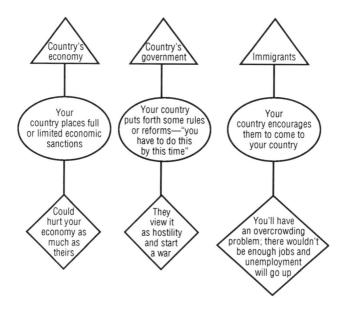

The ovals represent particular actions that these actors might perform. The diamonds represent constraints on these actions, elicited by a probe question: "Are there any problems with the solutions that you have suggested, any reasons that they might not work?"

The schemata of the international system implied by the adolescent whose response is graphed in Figure 1.1 were very rudimentary at the presession interview. This individual began by seeing a human rights violation, such as apartheid, as a matter for the United Nations to discuss. After the simulation, as represented in Figure 1.2, this respondent did not mention the United Nations but spoke instead of economic sanctions, demands for reform, and encouragement to immigrate for the groups being discriminated against. After the simulation, there are three actors, each with an action and a constraint. These changes can be characterized as a movement from pre-novice to novice over the course of the simulation.

The adolescent whose schema-maps appear in Figures 1.3 and 1.4 mentioned three actors ("your country, the other country, and your allies"), each with one action, before the simulation. Two of the actions were constrained, that is, reasons were given about why they might not work. After

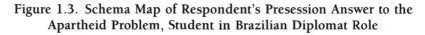

Figure 1.3. Schema Map of Respondent's Presession Answer to the Apartheid Problem, Student in Brazilian Diplomat Role

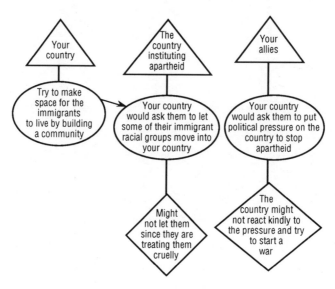

the simulation, there were seven actors, each with one or two actions. Only three constraints were mentioned. The presession represents a novice response, and the number of actors and actions mentioned in the postsession suggests classification as a post-novice. The absence of constraints and of connections between actions suggest that this adolescent has not yet reached the pre-expert phase.

This method seems to capture both continuity and restructuring of an individual's cognitive representations, as well as individual differences. For most respondents who participated in the foreign policy simulation, there was some similarity between the pre- and post-session interviews regarding the actors in the economic or political system who were mentioned and the actions that might be asked of them (compare Figures 1.1 and 1.2 and Figures 1.3 and 1.4). However, the schemata were clearly more complex after the simulation experience for the majority of students.

Some students saw only a few relatively rudimentary constraints. For example, a constraint on solutions to the finance minister's debt problem was that the banks might not agree to reduce the loans. Others not only saw many constraints but also connected them to each other, for example, "If you

Figure 1.4. Schema Map of Respondent's Postsession Answer to the Apartheid Problem, Student in Brazilian Diplomat Role

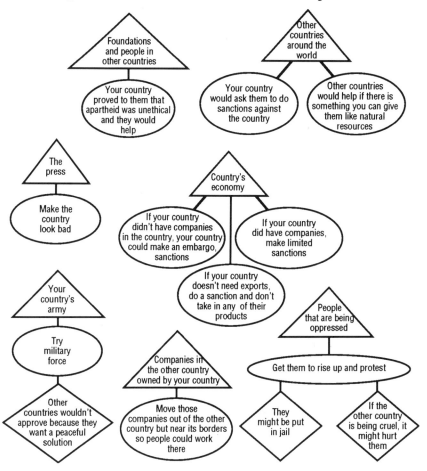

got together with other developing countries to refuse to pay, you might bankrupt the banks and that would have an impact on the world economy." Constraints in the apartheid problem included the difficulty of changing racial attitudes and policies and the possibility that economic sanctions, if enacted, would unintentionally hurt the racial minority. The ability to see the complexity of solutions to problems and not merely to think that requests for debt aid will always be answered or that a government contemplating apartheid laws can be convinced that they are unjust, are important aspects of a complex representation of the international system and an important part of the movement from novice to post-novice to pre-expert.

The difficulty that young people (novices and post-novices) had in dealing with constraints was especially obvious in their responses to the mayor's toxic waste problem. These responses were relatively impoverished with respect to the number of actors and actions mentioned. These young people also failed to deal with a major constraint stated in the problem: a decision requiring the company to clean up the waste might result in its going out of business and many jobs being lost to the town. The adolescents either ignored the polluting company and suggested nonpolitical alternatives such as organizing a local fair to raise money for cleanup or else dismissed the possible economic consequences to the town by saying that "loss of jobs is a small price to pay for loss of life." The "experts" almost always dealt with the problem of balancing solutions with constraints and making choices in the light of competing costs and benefits.

Most of the students in this group responded to the debt and the apartheid problems in ways that placed them at the novice or post-novice phase. (Post-novice responses were seen primarily in the postsession interviews.) However, most were categorized at the novice phase on the domestic toxic waste problem. The second group of students, those who participated in the educational program in Washington, D.C., were primarily at the pre-novice and novice phases. The large majority of the third group of respondents, the Coast Guard officials and group leaders, fit the pre-expert and expert categories for both domestic and international problems. Although the responses of the three groups were not evenly spread across the pre-novice to expert continuum, they do suggest the applicability of this approach to a broad range of expertise and the appropriateness of the continuum as a way of conceptualizing developmental change.

The integration of attitudes into cognitive structures was explored with questions about how the respondents felt about the problem of debt and the problem of apartheid. For many adolescents, feelings of outrage were associated with consequences for the racial minority in the event of apartheid laws. This attitudinal dimension requires further exploration.

Think-aloud problem solving has been described as a way to elicit the underlying cognitive representations of political and economic systems. When faced with a hypothetical political problem, adolescents draw on their domain-specific knowledge as organized in schemata of the political or economic system. The graphic schema-maps do not deal with the problem-solving process, a function of schemata identified by Rumelhart (1980) and investigated by Voss, Tyler, and Yengo (1983). However, the data discussed here suggest that one of the major contrasts between the responses of the adolescent novices and the experts was the way that the problem was approached, that is, the representation of what a political problem was and what it meant to solve it. Even the post-novice adolescents simply ran through possible pairs of actors and actions, usually saying, "I'd try . . . , then I'd try. . . ." Their strategy was similar to a trial-and-error approach to solving a math problem. Some of the students seemed to expect that the interviewer would tell them when they had stated the correct answer. In contrast, the experts nearly always began by developing a complex representation of the problem, often one that involved conflict. For example, the following two responses were given to the mayor's toxic waste problem: "This is obviously a problem of competing interests" and "This problem is based on a set of value judgments and the resolution of the problem becomes one of balancing short-term versus long-term values and coming to grips with the consequences." The experts discussing the finance minister's debt problem began by noting that they would have to know more about the developing country represented, as all developing countries were not the same in their resources or political characteristics. This use of schemata to set the stage for political problem solving deserves further exploration across the range of pre-novice to expert, with particular attention to the question of whether the content and the procedural schemata develop independently.

Discussion

A domain-specific framework for considering political socialization in terms of schemata or cognitive representations and their functions has been proposed. A continuum of political expertise, from pre-novice to expert, has been explored as a framework for the study of development. This continuum is a concrete way to apply insights of cognitive psychology to understand political development. It incorporates many observed changes in political understanding during adolescence. Pre-novices and novices have less elaborate or complex schemata for political, social, and economic systems and events than do those further along the continuum of expertise. They have less knowledge to retrieve because of lack of exposure to information and because of poor differentiation of the schemata needed to organize storage of that information. For example, McKeown and Beck (1990) refer to fifth graders' lack of ability to distinguish between the Constitution and the Bill of Rights; both are seen as important pieces of paper that have something to do with history or government, as part of a "document stew."

In addition, adolescent pre-novices and novices are limited in their cognitive resources. They do not spontaneously employ efficient cognitive strategies, for example, elaboration or organization of material that they read or hear. All of these characteristics of pre-novices and novices contribute to what adults perceive as a lack of maturity of political thought in adolescents.

Political maturity or expertise viewed in this way is the development of representations or schemata that serve functions in the learning and recall of information, the comprehension of discourse, and the solving of political problems. This approach represents a promising new direction in the study of political socialization, conceptualized as the study of expansion and differentiation in individuals' private understandings of politics in ways that make public issues meaningful and engaging.

References

Berti, A. E., and Bombi, A. S. *The Child's Construction of Economics.* Cambridge, England: Cambridge University Press, 1988.

Chi, M.T.H., Hutchinson, J., and Robin, A. "How Inferences About Novel Domain-Related Concepts Can Be Constrained by Structured Knowledge." *Merrill-Palmer Quarterly,* 1989, *35,* 27–62.

Duveen, G., and Lloyd, B. (eds.). *Social Representations and the Development of Knowledge.* Cambridge, England: Cambridge University Press, 1990.

Fiske, S., Lau, R., and Smith, R. "On the Varieties and Utilities of Political Expertise." *Social Cognition,* 1990, *8,* 31–48.

Graber, D. A. *Processing the News.* (2nd ed.) New York: Longman, 1988.

Hallden, O. "Learning History." *Oxford Review of Education,* 1986, *12,* 33–66.

Hayes, J. R. *The Complete Problem Solver.* Philadelphia: Franklin Institute Press, 1981.

Jennings, M. K., and Niemi, R. *Generations and Politics.* Princeton, N.J.: Princeton University Press, 1981.

McGraw, K., and Pinney, N. "The Effects of General and Domain-Specific Expertise on Political Memory and Judgment." *Social Cognition,* 1990, *8,* 9–30.

McKeown, M., and Beck, I. "The Assessment and Characterization of Young Learners' Knowledge of a Topic in History." *American Educational Research Journal,* 1990, 27 (4), 688–726.

Messick, D., and Mackie, D. "Intergroup Relations." *Annual Review of Psychology,* 1989, *40,* 45–82.

Moore, S., Lare, J., and Wagner, K. *The Child's Political World.* New York: Praeger, 1985.

Pratkanis, A. "The Cognitive Representation of Attitudes." In A. Pratkanis, S. Breckler, and A. Greenwald (eds.), *Attitudes Structure and Function.* Hillsdale, N.J.: Erlbaum, 1989.

Rumelhart, D. "Schemata: The Building Blocks of Cognition." In R. Spiro, B. Bruce, and W. Brewer (eds.), *Theoretical Issues in Reading Comprehension.* Hillsdale, N.J.: Erlbaum, 1980.

Torney-Purta, J. "Political Cognition and Its Restructuring in Young People." *Human Development,* 1989, *32,* 14–23.

Torney-Purta, J. "From Attitudes and Knowledge to Schemata: Expanding the Outcomes of Political Socialization." In O. Ichilov (ed.), *Political Socialization, Citizenship Education, and Democracy.* New York: Teachers College Press, 1990a.

Torney-Purta, J. "Youth in Relation to Social Institutions." In S. Feldman and G. Elliott (eds.), *At the Threshold: The Developing Adolescent.* Cambridge, Mass.: Harvard University Press, 1990b.

Tourangeau, R. "Attitude Measurement: A Cognitive Perspective." In H. Hippler, N. Schwarz, and S. Sudman (eds.), *Social Information Processing and Survey Methodology.* New York: Springer-Verlag, 1987.

Voss, J. F., Tyler, S., and Yengo, L. "Individual Differences in the Solving of Social Science Problems." In R. Dillon and R. Schmeck (eds.), *Individual Differences in Problem Solving.* San Diego, Calif.: Academic Press, 1983.

JUDITH TORNEY-PURTA is professor of human development and affiliate professor of psychology at the University of Maryland, College Park.

Socialization is viewed as a process of applying lay social theories to political, social, and personal issues among British adolescents.

Lay Social Theory: The Relation Between Political, Social, and Moral Understanding

Helen Haste

The young person enters into adulthood and citizenship with an array of beliefs relating to economic, social, and political issues. Explanations of the establishment of these beliefs differ. *Political socialization* models presume that beliefs and values transfer across generations and so seek parallels between developing attitudes and the map of adult political divisions. In contrast, the *cognitive developmental* approach concentrates on the developing understanding of economic and social issues, of how political systems function, and of the citizen's relationship to them; the individual actively makes sense of experience, generating an increasingly complex theory of how the world works.

This chapter argues that political development is a social process, but that the individual actively constructs meaning within a social context. Which particular concepts develop depends on the *available repertoire* of belief systems within a culture. An example of an available repertoire comes from Helen, a thirteen-year-old British adolescent who would vote Communist because she believes in equality: "I think everyone should be equal. And I don't believe in Christianity, or religion, I don't think there's any need to have those really." This statement may be shocking to readers in the United States, but the existence of varieties of Communist parties within the European political system makes Helen's position rare but not outrageous. On the other hand, there are forms of the religious right in the United States that have no real counterparts in Europe.

New Directions for Child Development, no. 56, Summer 1992 © Jossey-Bass Publishers

Lay Social Theory

Lay social theory, in essence, is a set of schemata and scenarios of how the world works and how the individual is located in that world. The term bridges the gap between those who concentrate on internal processes of thought and see any change as the outcome of individual restructuring, and those who emphasize the social nature of thought (Haste, 1992). Lay social theory is constituted by schemata and scenarios, which explain or account for origin or cause, imply a desired goal or state, define what is salient in a situation, provide a structure for seeing logical relations between salient aspects, and, finally, delineate appropriate responses to the situation. A key element of lay social theory is the assumption about what works and why. An example is the belief that strong punishment is important in dealing with criminals. In traditional terms, this is an attitude with an affective component. But considered as a scenario of what works, it involves schemata about deterrence, revenge, or protection of society from further violence.

Lay social theory is not confined to the explicitly political domain. A distinction can be made between the political and other areas of life: morality, personal relationships, and ordinary interaction with institutions. Yet, adolescents as young as twelve reveal a lively interest in the social issues that underlie the political domain and that serve to distinguish party policies, for example, unemployment, crime, welfare provision, and forms of power sharing. These issues have salience because they affect people in their everyday lives.

Lay social theory assumes that the individual is active in constructing meaning and making sense of experience, but that these processes take place within the set of lay social theories available in the culture; use of lay social theories depends on constant negotiation of meaning in discourse with others, who clarify, evaluate, and legitimate concepts. The culture makes certain things salient rather than others, provides explanations, and defines what is problematic and what is not. Culturally constituted and shared meanings concern not only what is known and understood but also what is seen as *necessary* to know and to justify. Much cognitive activity, especially about social issues, is a matter of public discourse rather than private reflection, and it requires strategies for effective public communication, not merely the ability to grasp concepts. Billig (1987) argues that social psychology has traditionally assumed that people arrive at their conclusions by a form of logic, and that where conflicts arise, people tend to reduce them, seeking consistency. But, in fact, people hold apparently conflicting views that constitute their own personal repertoire of responses; in discourse they use whatever rhetoric seems most effective in putting across their viewpoints. This means that we must look not only at what people say but also at what their arguments implicitly oppose or justify.

There are two traditions about how to arrive at truth. In one, it is through logic that the individual arrives at a single, best solution. The alternative, rhetorical tradition is that truth is reached through argumentation and the conflict of different points of view—necessarily a social process. An essential element is what is deemed a matter for dispute. Some things are seen as problematic, others are taken for granted. Something that is seen as problematic is explained differently from something that is taken for granted. The former requires an explanation, or a resolution, of the unusual; whereas the latter, the taken for granted or the usual, if questioned at all, is explained in terms of its functional inevitability. The young individual picks up from the media, and from ordinary conversations, concepts about what is problematic and what is taken for granted, and what are perceived to be the common and acceptable solutions and explanations.

To understand what is problematic and what is taken for granted, it is necessary to see how the salient issues are embedded in explanations. For example, for Helen, the Communist, the concept of equality is important, and she also rejects religion; to understand her lay social theory we need more information about how equality and antisecularism are salient themes in other areas of her thinking, and how she has identified the Communist party with those themes. For Brian, another youth in my study sample, moderation and centralism are salient. Brian supported the Social Democrats: "They're not so left wing, and they're not right wing. They're sort of in the center, they're just the right sort of grade."

Case Studies of Lay Social Theories

The four case studies presented here—Brian, Helen, Adrian, and Karen—are drawn from a study of British adolescents. The interviewer used a combination of semistructured questions and hypothetical situations. This method requires respondents to present explicitly his or her repertoire of problem-solving schemata. Hypothetical situations and areas of ambiguity such as "Can you think of a time when you weren't sure what was the right thing to do?" require respondents to interpret events and reveal what they see as problematic. One of the hypothetical situations used was an adaptation of the Islanders story developed by Adelson and O'Neil (1966), a story originally designed to tap the respondents' understanding of democracy by asking them to consider the hypothetical scenario of a group marooned on a desert island and faced with social and political problems. The present study asked about the problems that the islanders encountered and their solutions. Responses reveal assumptions about social order and ways of resolving conflict. The study also used Kohlberg's moral dilemmas (Colby and Kohlberg, 1987).

Lay social theories are revealed in common themes that emerge across wide areas of life experience; they are manifestations of personal repertoires of schemata. Individuals also demonstrate recurrent procedures for organizing their argumentation and justification. These organizing principles underlie the interpretation of experience, affect the choice of schemata and what is justified and how, and express what is taken-for-granted and what is problematic. In the present study, three dimensions emerged as organizing principles for lay social theory.

The first dimension involves Gilligan's (1982) and Gilligan, Ward, and Taylor's (1988) distinctions between two orientations to interpersonal and moral relations, which reflect differences in how relations between people are perceived. The *connected* orientation perceives relations in terms of interdependency. Conflict resolution requires cooperation and negotiation; negotiation, cooperation, and compromise are, in the terms of lay social theory, *what work* for achieving the desirable state of harmony. In the *separate* orientation, people are conceptualized as isolated and in conflict with others; the solution is to make contracts or rules for fair outcomes, or to prevent further problems. Rules and codes are what work. The present study of British adolescents identified the separate-connected distinction in several areas, not only in relation to moral issues and relationships (Wingfield and Haste, 1987; Haste and Baddeley, 1991).

The second dimension involves the distinction between *collectivist* and *individualistic* perspectives. Collectivist thinking locates the origins of social problems in economic and social forces, and their solutions in large-scale policy changes. Individualistic thinking locates the origins of social problems in individual foibles or deficiencies, and their solutions in changes directed toward individual behavior (Feather, 1974; Furnham, 1982).

The third dimension involves the distinction between *advocacy* and *deliberation,* which arises from Billig's (1987) discussion of how rhetoric is used and how inconsistencies are resolved in discourse. Advocacy is the presentation of one point of view, with the expectation that the other person will present the alternative position. Deliberation is the presentation of alternative points of view by one person; the debate is presented as internal. These two styles have far-reaching effects on how young people acquire and use schemata. Advocates are, in effect, holding in mind—or, at least, in discourse—only one schema at a time, whether in anticipation of the need to defend it or as a way of sustaining subjective consistency. Deliberators move between alternatives, recognizing the existence of several points of view at once.

The four cases here show cross-domain patterns of theme and explanation. They illustrate the interweaving of recurrent schemata and scenarios, reflecting the application of a common lay social theory in disparate areas of moral, social, and political reasoning. They also show, first, how the organizing principles of the three dimensions recur, and, second, how these organizing principles, which in effect have the characteristics of cognitive style, feed into the schemata and scenarios, framing perception and making some things salient.

Brian. Brian, age thirteen, wants to follow his father into the navy. For him, law, order, and social structure are problematic. This viewpoint was very clear in his discussion of school rules:

INTERVIEWER: Do you think school rules are important?
BRIAN: Yes, otherwise nothing will get done, if everybody did what they wanted to, it would just be sort of haywire, everyone going anywhere, missing lessons. Rules keep people in order.

He has a collectivist perspective; rules sustain the social system, and continuing unemployment would contribute to social breakdown through its effect on individual morale:

BRIAN: If unemployment goes on as it is going, people might get into that habit of thinking, well, if it's never going to stop, we might as well goof about. . . . If that goes on for another twenty years, they'll start to get more degrading social attitudes; you know, if you're unemployed, and your father's something, well that puts you in a different set to if your father's unemployed and you're working—puts you in a higher set or a lower set.
INTERVIEWER: What will be the consequences of that?
BRIAN: Rebellion, in a way, a bit of rebellion. I'm not saying on a violent scale, but the whole society will start to fall and crumble.

His concern with order underlies his view that the Islanders needed good planning and morale:

INTERVIEWER: What kinds of things do you think were happening?
BRIAN: Rivalry between the individuals that previously went off to make a living, almost a civil war but not quite. The rivalry might have been caused by lack of some of the resources . . . some groups wanting other resources so they'd overpower the other groups, and that would cause rebellion.
INTERVIEWER: How can they go about solving their problems?
BRIAN: Probably they'd divide up the land into equal sections and give a certain plot of land to every person or family. Food problem, distribution of resources to each group. To stop the rivalry, maybe splitting the groups apart, and maybe taking one or two people from each group and making a sort of police force.

Brian is a deliberator, and he accommodates alternative perspectives. In his response to the question of why people ought to obey the law, both a collectivist perspective and a tempering deliberation are evident:

INTERVIEWER: So what do you think is the purpose of the law?

BRIAN: To keep society together.

INTERVIEWER: Do you think it's ever right to break the law?

BRIAN: If the law's laid down, I believe it should be stuck to. Full stop. But on humanitarian grounds [for example, in the dilemma of a man who must choose to steal a drug or watch his wife die] I'd say, go ahead, I'd help you.

One reflection of Brian's deliberator style is that he often puts forward alternative positions; he continually recognizes the possibility of disagreement, and the existence of factions or sectors of society who disagree with a given point of view. This potential for disagreement is taken into consideration in resolving unemployment, in making school more democratic, in eliminating crime, and in teaching religious education. In the latter case, although a practicing Christian, he observes that the existence of many different points of view on religion makes religious education inappropriate.

Two striking examples of his deliberator style involve his response to the Joe Dilemma. The Joe Dilemma is one of Kohlberg's moral reasoning stories. It concerns a boy who earns money to go to a school camp after his father has promised that he can, and then the father asks Joe for the money for his own purposes. The question is whether Joe should refuse his father, or lie about how much he earned. In responding to this story, Brian attends to both elements, two sets of schemata. On the one hand, he draws on the schema that Joe earned it, it is his by right: "It came from his own time and sweat, and his effort to get the money, whereas his father, he didn't have anything to do with it." On the other hand—and he does not really resolve the dilemma—he argues as follows: "He shouldn't really give the father the money, because the father promised Joe that he could keep the money and go to camp, but his father is the head of the family, the financial part of the family, and keeps the family going, earning money for the food, I think he should, plus I think he should look up to his parents. . . . I'd give the money to my father because well, one, he's my father, and two, I think I'd know he'd be doing best. . . . That money was totally his really, but he should be faithful to his mother and father."

Brian is distinctly separate in his views of relationships. In the question about keeping promises, connected responses emphasize mutual trust between friends, and how the relationship would be affected by breaking that trust. Separate responses focus on the quality of personal integrity of the promise keeper; Brian is an example of the latter: "A promise is important because it shows that you've got to be faithful to the person. When you make a promise you'll do what the promise is, what you've drawn up and you'll keep your word on it. You've put yourself in that position by saying yourself that you'll keep the promise."

Brian is a collectivist deliberator with a separate orientation to relationships; he looks for ways to create order and rules that steer a course of moderation and minimize conflict.

Helen. Helen, age thirteen, views the Communist party as the party of antisecularism and equality. For her, the problematic issues are equality and individual freedom. With respect to family life in the future, she says the following: "Hopefully things will be more equal, there will be more opportunities for people. I think it will be better, like in the home, the man won't have his jobs and the woman have her job, they won't be separate, they'll just share things. Like the woman won't always be expected to do the washing up and do the cooking and the man won't always be expected to mend the plugs and things." She sees the Islanders as free to start afresh, from a position of equality: "If they were all marooned on the island they would all be equal, so they ought to pick [the council members] at random; just pick anybody."

For Helen, royalty are an example of the antithesis of egalitarianism: "There's all the money being spent on them and they don't do anything except go round and shake hands with people. So there's really no use having them. I mean any family could be chosen to do that. What is so special about them? And all the money that they have could be shared out among the people." Moreover, her concern with individual freedom has led to relativism and libertarianism: "It's up to people to make their own minds up. If they want to kill themselves by smoking, let them."

A question about obeying the law showed how she embeds this obedience in her beliefs about how the law works:

HELEN: No, I just think there is no use obeying the law. People don't obey it anyway. Like they say you're not allowed to record from the radio, everybody in the country must record from the radio. People just don't take any notice of most of the rules. They're useless, they don't help our economy or anything; I don't think they do any good really.

INTERVIEWER: Any of them?

HELEN: Well, some. I think they should have rules but . . . if you break them you shouldn't get put in prison, or charge you or anything. . . . If you murder someone it's different, but if you drive a car and you're drunk, well it's up to you, it's your fault.

Helen's collectivist orientation comes out in her views on unemployment: "I think [the government] should be trying to create more jobs instead of just putting people on new training schemes, and half of them haven't got anywhere to go afterwards."

Helen is an advocate, which leads her to contradict herself. When Brian recognizes that he holds conflicting views, he deliberates; however, Helen switches her advocacy according to the situation. In fact, when asked about general rules and about reasons for having rules, it is clear that she only considers laws to be breakable when they do not affect anyone else. Her response to the Islanders story makes this viewpoint clear. She sees the problem the Islanders had as one of community and cooperation, a view that reflects a connected orientation:

> People were stealing from other people; the people were just doing things for themselves, and not helping anyone else. So they probably just thought they ought to be more organized, so they'd be more like a team, more like a community. Instead of spreading out over the island, try to make like a capital. All go to one place on the island and just try to settle down. Make like a leader and make some rules up then, because that's the time when they would need them. Then, when things got better, maybe you could abolish the rules or put them out of use, because people will know what's happening anyway.

Helen has well-established—if somewhat confused—schemata about laws and rules, and about equality. She is an advocate rather than a deliberator; she presents one point of view and expects it to be countered by others. And where she does hold contradictory or inconsistent views (as in the case of rules and law), she presents one picture or the other, without seeing them explicitly as problematic.

Adrian. Adrian, age seventeen, would vote Conservative and wants to become a merchant banker. His primary schemata concern law, order, and rules, and his scenarios concern ways to maintain these through forms of control and planning: "You've got to have laws to keep the system together. If murder wasn't illegal, then people would just go around pushing each other's faces in. It's one of the things that keeps society together, part of democracy." This general theme is echoed in his discussion of the Islanders' need for laws to maintain control: "They'd have to make sure that they worked together, so there was no sort of hassle, aggro, like stealing the other man's woman. And basic rules of safety." Moreover, through school rules, according to Adrian, the growing individual learns moral controls: "It's a good way to condition people for when they leave school, because you're going to have rules basically throughout your life, in your job, whatever, so it gets you used to them."

Adrian's view of order is based on the importance of planning, structure, and hierarchy rather than on unbridled chaos. The Islanders' order depended on expertise. Their main problem is the distribution of resources; Adrian's solution is structured leadership: "I think they'd be better off organized together, with one or a group of leaders. People with leadership qualities, people with skills, knowledge. You would assume that there would be one person or so who would be able to take command. Say there'd been a captain, somebody who had had authority beforehand."

He has, in general, a collectivist approach to unemployment and crime, but he also uses individualistic explanations, as in the following statements on the causes of unemployment:

> Increasing technology, and we've got the whole world depression at the moment. Maybe people aren't educated in the right fields. I think a bit more government spending might be useful. . . . The people who I know who are unemployed, basically, they could do a lot more about it. I find the ones I know are very lazy, and they just can't be bothered to write off, just on the off chance they might get a job. They went straight on the dole or a Youth Training Scheme, but most of them I know are single-parent families and they just haven't been brought up to think about it, you know?

Adrian has a separate orientation that emphasizes codes and the conflict between codes when talking about relationships; a "difficult decision" for him concerns the following situation: "Splitting [tattling] on a friend. You've got loyalty to a friend, and there again, you've got the law. Personally, I deplore drugs but a lot of the kids I know smoke dope and take speed, and I feel I should split on them, but it's just not right, it's not the thing." In talking about keeping promises, he focuses on the qualities of self rather than on the relationship: "If you say you're going to do something, and you don't do it, then it's not going to make people want to trust you, or believe in you, or rely on you at all. It's basically for your own pride . . . how you feel to yourself."

Adrian is an advocate rather than a deliberator, but he rarely contradicts himself, in contrast with Helen. He shows a separate rather than connected orientation across virtually all of his thinking. He draws on collectivist understanding but nevertheless explains some social order in terms of personal virtue.

Karen. Karen, age fifteen, would vote Labour. For her, the maintenance of relationships and communication are most problematic. A key element of Karen's thinking is listening; it recurs often in her language. As Gilligan (1982) points out, listening is a central element of the connected orientation. In the Islanders story, Karen exemplifies the connected stress on the communication between the Islanders:

> Get together and have a meeting, talk, arrange something so that they can all have the same, instead of one group having more than the other. Perhaps they could choose a leader between the different sides of the island, and they go together, have a meeting, and then go back and tell the others. Different groups would have to select the one that they thought is most reliable, who would say the truth. Everyone has to say their point, but the one who's most liked—maybe a few lower down as well, and not so liked, because they're never going to get listened to by anybody.

As well as listening, the connected orientation emphasizes avoidance of hurt. For Karen, promise keeping is associated with hurt avoidance, rather than with the quality of the promise: "You can hurt people's feelings as well and then they just rebel, and both sides get hurt. And if they'd thought about it, then no one's feelings would be hurt."

Listening is also embedded in Karen's version of deliberation, which is apparent in her view of the Islanders and of the importance of dealing with alternative points of view. Karen recognizes hierarchies of persuasion, which integrate her schemata of listening and her awareness of alternative perspectives: "Different people, what they think, I suppose. As soon as the higher ones think of something, then all the lower people think, 'Well, that's right, and we'll follow that.' . . . And there are people who just don't agree with it—there's always two sides to everything, no matter what it is, there'll always be two sides. So those people, if they're following someone higher up, then they'll tell other people, and they'll probably agree with them, and it will just go on like that." Her account of uncertainty about "the right thing to do" specifically concerns the negotiation of competing viewpoints and the possibility of hurt—the integration of connectedness and deliberation: "Split up between friends, and you're not sure which one to go to. We'd been together, a three, and the other two had broken up, and you're in the middle, and you don't know which way to go. If you go one way, you've upset the other one, and if you go the other way, you've upset the first one. I hate that situation."

Her appreciation of the perspective of others is particularly well illustrated in her response to the Louise Dilemma, the female version of the Joe Dilemma. In this story, the central question is whether Louise should tell their mother that her sister Judy has lied about the money that she earned to go to a rock concert: "I don't know. Louise might tell her because she knows that her sister did wrong, but there again she might not have seen her sister's point of view when she said that—one minute she said yes and the next minute she said no."

Karen has an individualistic rather than a collectivist perspective on rules and laws. Her attitude toward school rules is that they keep people under control, but she is vociferous that they should be changed if people do not agree with them. She differs from the other three respondents in that her lay social theories are deeply embedded in relationships and communication, rather than in rules, codes, or authority.

Conclusion

These four case studies show how individuals use common schemata, and similar principles for organizing concepts, across very different areas of their social and political experience. Each person has interwoven an externally derived, socially constructed understanding of issues such as crime, political parties, and authority with more personal schemata deriving from direct experience and interaction. Karen recurrently used listening as her scenario for what works in many different areas. Her orientation in relationships was connected, and she was a deliberator who mainly focused on individualistic aspects of the situation. All of these dimensions contributed to her lay social theory of sociopolitical interaction as the cooperative negotiation of different interests aimed toward the most harmonious solution. Brian was also a deliberator, but with a collectivist perspective and a separate orientation. He also wanted to find ways of dealing with competing points of view, but for him rules and codes governed the process and those attributes that allow people to trust and keep faith. For Adrian, a separate advocate who combined a collectivist understanding with a preference for attributing much to individual characteristics, order and control at both the societal and the individual levels were important. Rules and codes were the source of this control and of the application of expertise. Finally, for Helen, her collectivist perspective combined with her schema of equality and liberty to give her a picture of society as oppressive, whereas for both Brian and Adrian a collectivist view of society was a source of structure and order. Her advocacy style made her, like Adrian, confrontational, but for him this advocacy translated into a general awareness of conflict. Helen showed a mixture of separate and connected thought; her advocacy style and her sense of injustice mitigated somewhat against negotiation, but in the Islanders situation she saw the solution more in terms of connection and cooperation; her schemata of equality and liberty led her to see what works in terms of a community of equals who did not need laws. But she, like Adrian, thought there was a necessary period of rule making and order.

The implication of these examples for a model of development is, foremost, that political reasoning is not separate from other domains. The young individual may acquire particular beliefs or values from parents, the school, or other indirect sources of cultural legitimation, but he or she interprets them and integrates them into a set of schemata that are used across a wide range of experiences and issues. This wide applicability of schemata demonstrates the extent to which even thirteen-year-olds can construct subjectively coherent worldviews and utilize similar schemata in different contexts. This finding is consistent with cognitive developmental theory. But a model of lay social theory emphasizes also the cultural context; these adolescents were incorporating, selectively, recognizable and legitimated schemata and scenarios that are extant within British culture. They were constructing their own meanings, making sense of their political and social world, but only by drawing on a socially constructed resource of available lay social theory.

References

Adelson, J., and O'Neil, R. "The Growth of Political Ideas in Adolescence: The Sense of Community." *Journal of Personality and Social Psychology*, 1966, *4*, 295–306.

Billig, M. *Arguing and Thinking*. Cambridge, England: Cambridge University Press, 1987.

Colby, A., and Kohlberg, L. *The Measurement of Moral Judgement*. Cambridge, England: Cambridge University Press, 1987.

Feather, N. T. "Explanations of Poverty in Australian and American Samples: The Person, Society or Fate?" *Australian Journal of Psychology*, 1974, *26*, 199–216.

Furnham, A. "Explanations for Unemployment in Britain." *European Journal of Social Psychology*, 1982, *12*, 335–352.

Gilligan, C. *In a Different Voice: Psychological Theory and Women's Development*. Cambridge, Mass.: Harvard University Press, 1982.

Gilligan, C., Ward, J. V., and Taylor, J. M. *Mapping the Moral Domain*. Cambridge, Mass.: Harvard University Press, 1988.

Haste, H. "Morality, Self, and Sociohistorical Context: The Role of Lay Social Theory." In G. Noam and T. Wren (eds.), *Morality and the Self*. Cambridge, Mass.: MIT Press, 1992.

Haste, H., and Baddeley, J. "Moral Theory and Culture: The Case of Gender." In J. Gewirtz and W. Kurtines (eds.), *Handbook of Moral Behavior and Development*. Hillsdale, N.J.: Erlbaum, 1991.

Wingfield, L., and Haste, H. "Connectedness and Separateness: Cognitive Style or Moral Orientation?" *Journal of Moral Education*, 1987, *16*, 214–225.

HELEN HASTE is senior lecturer in psychology, University of Bath, England.

The socialization of political tolerance is influenced by U.S.
adolescents' conceptualizations of dissent and dissenters.

Political Tolerance: How Adolescents Deal with Dissenting Groups

Patricia G. Avery

Among liberal democratic theorists, tolerance for diversity of belief is considered fundamental to the sustenance of a democratic society. Students of U.S. political socialization and education have documented the disparity between support for abstract democratic principles (for example, freedom of assembly) and support for their application to concrete situations (for example, a Ku Klux Klan rally). For more than three decades, scholars have investigated the role of political tolerance in society, scrutinized variables that may predict tolerance, and argued whether levels of tolerance are increasing or decreasing (Sullivan, Pierson, and Marcus, 1982; Stouffer, 1955).

Research questions and methodologies, however, have remained limited in scope. Most of the research on political tolerance has focused on quantitative analysis of responses to paper-and-pencil attitude instruments. People typically are asked to indicate their agreement with items such as "If a person wanted to make a speech in this city against churches and religion, he or she should be allowed to speak" or "A citizen should be allowed to appear on television to campaign for a Nazi party candidate."

While survey data allow us to focus on specific variables, the nature of survey items generally fails to capture the complex dimensions of political tolerance. Freedom of expression and assembly have never been absolute. As Justice Oliver Wendell Holmes said, "The most stringent protection of free speech would not protect a man in falsely shouting fire in a theatre and causing panic" (*Schenck* v. *United States*, 249 U.S. 47 [1919]). By decon-

Financial support for the research reported here came from the Graduate School of the University of Minnesota and is gratefully acknowledged.

textualizing rights issues, traditional survey items present questions on this topic as essentially unproblematic.

The interpretation of survey responses introduces yet another dilemma. A "tolerant" response may indicate apathy rather than support for freedom of expression. Conversely, persons may support the democratic principle and still give an "intolerant" response. Suppose an individual denies free speech to a political group because the group has previously denied freedom of expression to others. The person reasons that if the group were to assume power, it would mean restrictions on free speech for a greater number of people. In this case, the person values freedom of expression but reasons that the principle is better protected in the long run by denying such expression to a few. Assumptions about respondents' reasoning may therefore obscure rather than enhance our understanding of political tolerance.

The present study moves beyond traditional survey items and explores some of the more complex issues related to political tolerance. It is proposed that tolerance judgments are linked to one's conceptualization of dissent and dissenters. Survey and interview data are combined to portray a small sample of tolerant and intolerant youth.

Adolescents and Political Tolerance

Adolescence is an important time to capture students' voices as they struggle with issues related to rights and responsibilities. The nexus between personal and political identity formation during this period has been described by Erikson (1968) and Adams (1985). Political problems and issues provide adolescents with opportunities to explore and test evolving personal belief systems.

The emerging capacity for abstract thought processes enables the adolescent to consider the implications of specific acts for the individual and society and to connect abstract principles with concrete situations (Adelson, 1971). Also, group-related attitudes, often a critical dimension of tolerance, crystallize during adolescence and tend to persist through adulthood (Miller and Sears, 1986). Each of these processes has particular import in situations that ask individuals to accord rights to sociopolitical groups who may be unpopular or disliked.

Despite the interesting opportunities that adolescence offers for an exploration of the dimensions of tolerance, far fewer studies have been conducted with youth than with adults. What is known about adolescent political tolerance?

First, similar to adults, the more negative adolescents' perceptions of a group, the less likely they are to extend rights to the group (Avery, 1988; Owen and Dennis, 1987; Zellman and Sears, 1971). This is perhaps the most consistent finding of research on both adolescents and adults. Studies with adults have just begun to differentiate between the cognitive and affective bases of these perceptions (Marcus, Sullivan, and Theiss-Morse, 1990).

Second, young people who have been involved in formal political or quasi-political experiences are likely to be more tolerant than are those without this kind of experience (Avery, 1988; Jones, 1980). Political experiences appear to expose the individual to a wide range of opinions and attitudes, thereby increasing tolerance for the diversity of beliefs. Both developmental processes and social learning are relevant. Exposure to different viewpoints facilitates role taking, thus increasing the individual's understanding of various opinions. Similarly, those involved in politics often witness the respectful exchange of ideas.

Third, political tolerance has been found to be positively associated with one's level of moral reasoning (Avery, 1988; Patterson, 1979). Kohlberg's theory of cognitive moral development suggests that persons at the conventional level of reasoning demonstrate a sociocentric and legalistic orientation toward rights. Because rights are perceived as those agreed upon by the majority, individual or minority group rights may be given little consideration. At the postconventional level, rights such as freedom of expression are considered fundamental to human dignity and individual freedom (Kohlberg, 1981).

Finally, older adolescents tend to be more tolerant than their younger counterparts (Jones, 1980; Owen and Dennis, 1987). The transition from concrete to formal operational thought, which increases the likelihood of political involvement, appears to contribute to higher levels of political tolerance.

With few exceptions (Patterson, 1979), studies of adolescent political tolerance have been limited to survey methodology. While we are beginning to identify variables associated with political tolerance, we know little of how young people think about dissenting groups in society. A more complex understanding of political tolerance involves knowledge not only of whether persons extend rights to dissident groups but also of how they explain their decisions. In addition to keeping track of which "outcast" groups people dislike, we need to know how they account for the existence of these groups; we thus need to examine not only attitudes toward but also conceptions of dissent and dissenters.

This chapter examines how a small group of adolescents deal with dissenting sociopolitical groups. A central focus is the comparison of tolerant and intolerant students' perceptions of dissent and dissenters, with particular emphasis on their least-liked sociopolitical groups.

Method

The study consisted of two parts. In the first, students completed a written questionnaire designed to measure political tolerance; demographic, experiential, and attitudinal data were also obtained. In the second, a small number of these students were interviewed. The interviews gave the students an opportunity to voice their perceptions and concerns related to dissent and dissenters, without constraints and beyond the limits of predetermined responses. I focus here primarily on the interview data, in part because the literature has been dominated by survey research and in part because the interview data provide a richer understanding of the dimensions of tolerance. The survey format is described and the survey data are examined to the degree that they help to delineate the framework of the study.

The Survey: Measurement of Political Tolerance. A reconceptualization of political tolerance put forth by Sullivan, Piereson, and Marcus (1982) questioned the validity of previous research. They reasoned that tolerance requires simultaneous dislike and willingness to extend rights. One is not "tolerant" of a group's rights simply if one supports its goals. Hence, the measurement of political tolerance must take into account an individual's orientations toward various groups. Questions related to free speech and assembly, for example, should be directly tied to an individual's least-liked group. Previous studies had simply concentrated on whether persons would support a speech or rally led by a particular "outgroup" (usually Communists). Although not all researchers support Sullivan, Piereson, and Marcus's reconceptualization (Sniderman and others, 1989), the research has renewed interest and debate about the nature and complexity of political tolerance.

In the present study, political tolerance was defined as the willingness to extend human rights to one's least-liked sociopolitical group. The measurement of political tolerance on the survey consisted of two parts. In the first section, respondents were asked to select their least-liked sociopolitical group from a list of eleven outcast or dissident groups, or to name another group if appropriate. The second part consisted of twelve statements based on rights delineated in the Universal Declaration of Human Rights; students were asked whether they would be willing to extend these rights to their respectively specified least-liked groups. Each statement was followed by a 5-point Likert scale, ranging from "strongly agree" to "strongly disagree." Instrument reliability, as estimated by Cronbach's alpha, was .90.

Sample. In spring 1989, 564 tenth- and eleventh-grade students from two midwestern suburban high schools completed the questionnaire. The areas in which the schools are located were predominantly white and middle to upper-middle class. Approximately 75 percent of the graduates from each of the schools continue on with some form of formal education. Respondents included 306 males and 258 females; the mean age was 16.1 years.

Two weeks after the administration of the survey, twenty-two of the "most tolerant" and twenty-two of the "least tolerant" students (students among the top and bottom 6 percent of total scores on the survey's tolerance scale) participated in a semistructured interview. All interviewees were white, U.S. citizens. Data from the survey indicated that although the tolerant students tended to report higher grade-point averages, more extensive newspaper reading, and higher levels of political experiences, the differences were not statistically significant. Consistent with previous studies, the intolerant students indicated significantly more negative perceptions of their least-liked group (p = .022).

Ninety-one percent of the students gave consistently tolerant or intolerant responses on both the survey and the interview. Because one of the primary purposes of the study design was to compare tolerant and intolerant responses, students who were not classified similarly on both instruments were eliminated from the analysis of the interview data. The final interview sample consisted of twenty-one tolerant (ten females and eleven males) and eighteen intolerant students (four females and fourteen males). One interview with an intolerant student was later eliminated when it was discovered that she was a naturalized U.S. citizen. There was a similar proportion of females and males in the top and bottom 6 percent of the survey sample in terms of level of political tolerance.

Interview. At the beginning of the interview, students were given eleven cards, each with the name of one sociopolitical group typed on it. Students were each asked to rank the groups from their "most-liked group" to their "least-liked group." The interview in each case focused on the least-liked sociopolitical group. Questions such as "How would you describe the group to a friend who knew nothing about the group?" and "Why do you suppose someone might join the group?" were designed to probe students' perceptions of their least-liked sociopolitical groups. Interviews were conducted at the students' schools; the length of the interviews ranged from fifteen to twenty-five minutes. Two graduate research assistants, trained in interviewing techniques, interviewed the students. All interviews were taped and transcribed verbatim.

Analyzing the Data. The interview protocols were coded in an inductive manner informed by theory and past research. Categories were formed on the basis of perceived patterns of ideas or themes within responses to a given question. Thirty percent of the responses to each question were randomly selected and coded by another researcher; intercoder agreement ranged from .80 to 1.00.

Results

The interviews are presented to illustrate differences between tolerant and intolerant respondents' images of the group itself, of possible motives for joining, and of views of a rally in which it might participate.

Group Descriptions. When asked how they might describe their least-liked groups to a friend, the majority of both tolerant and intolerant students included evaluative comments in their descriptions (61 percent and 71 percent, respectively). Tolerant and intolerant students alike characterized their least-liked groups as "inhumane," "ruthless," "terrible," and "sick."

Nonevaluative descriptions, however, portrayed a different picture. These responses—coded in terms of the categories beliefs, actions, and historical references—represented a more objective orientation toward the groups than did the evaluative comments alone. The tolerant students were significantly more likely than the intolerant students to include objective references within their descriptions (94 percent versus 64 percent, respectively). Compare the following two descriptions of Nazis, the first from a tolerant female eleventh-grade student and the second from an intolerant male tenth-grade student: "The first thing that comes to mind is a political group based in Germany in World War II. Hum, it was cruel . . . didn't give any rights to the Jews. Caused a lot of pain and suffering for a lot of people. It's not a group I really like a lot." "Um, bad group of people, uh, their beliefs and political views, that's wrong, I think. I'd tell him not to get involved at all with them. And that's about it."

Although neither description provides detailed information, the first provides some contextual data, whereas the second is dominated by the student's evaluative comments. While it cannot be concluded that the intolerant students are unaware of their least-liked groups' beliefs, behaviors, or places in history, they are less likely to include these aspects in their descriptions. In essence, tolerant students are more likely to place their evaluations within a broader ideological or behavioral context.

Joining the Group. Why do students believe that someone would join their respective least-liked groups? Studies of attribution suggest that when behavior is negative and the group is an outgroup, individuals tend to make dispositional as opposed to situational attributions to account for the behavior (Stephan, 1977). The students in the present sample in fact cited three times more internal as opposed to external reasons for persons joining the groups and usually did so in an unreflective way: "Because they [antiabortionists] agree with the points made. That there should not be abortions." "They believe in what they [the Nazis] stand for, I guess." As Adelson (1971) found in his cross-national interviews with youth on social issues and problems, an appreciation of complex dimensions of human motivation in political situations is still beyond the realm of most of these adolescents' understanding.

Among those students who mentioned external or situational reasons for joining the groups, tolerant students were more likely than intolerant students to suggest the influence of family, friends, or specific experiences as the cause of behavior (38 percent versus 29 percent, respectively). Although slight, we can again see a trend in the responses of the tolerant students toward seeing the individual or group within a broad context.

To Rally or Not to Rally. When Gibson and Bingham (1983) asked members of the American Civil Liberties Union and Common Cause why they would or would not support the Nazis' request to march in Skokie, Illinois, in 1977, 90 percent of those supporting the Nazis' request cited the First Amendment as the basis of their reasoning. Responses from the tolerant students in the present study were strikingly similar: 90 percent mentioned the Constitution, the right to assemble, or the right to freedom of speech. Fifty-two percent of the tolerant students offered generalizations indicating that everyone has these rights. A tolerant male eleventh grader said, "Because *anyone should be allowed,* you know, because isn't . . . I thought that was like the Constitution says, you know, anyone should have the right to do . . . you know, that's their [the Ku Klux Klan's] right to go hold a rally and, you know, if it isn't hurting nothing, I don't see nothing wrong with it." A tolerant male tenth grader said, "I say they [the Nazis] could, as long as they maintain a peaceful demonstration. Cause *everybody is allowed to speak* . . . under the Constitution. . . . They're allowed their rights" (emphasis added). Generalizations such as these suggest that the students have an appreciation of the broader applications of freedom of expression and assembly.

The tolerant students linked the hypothetical situation to a legal norm, but it is uncertain whether they considered the norm's rationale. For example, among liberal democratic theorists, the expression of divergent viewpoints is thought to increase the stability of the political system by providing outlets for dissent, to further the search for "truth," and to meet the human need for self-expression (Corbett, 1982). Although students were probed as to whether they could offer additional reasons for allowing the rally, they were not asked why they considered "freedom of expression" important. Still, the fact that none of the interviewees elaborated much beyond general references to "freedom of speech" and the Constitution leads one to question the degree to which they have contemplated such issues. As Sigel and Hoskin (1981) found in their study of adolescent political involvement, young people are generally cognizant of the "slogans of democracy," but few appear to grapple with the attendant implications for society.

In the present study, an unexpected finding was that 90 percent of the tolerant students *qualified* their support for the rally. An eleventh-grade female said that the Ku Klux Klan could rally as long as they did not "have the meeting inside a black community." A tolerant female tenth-grade student felt that the community should have the opportunity to hear the opposing view: "I'd say, yea, go ahead, let 'em. But I'd also say that they should have an abortionist rally there at the same time . . . not at the same time, but they should have an antiabortionist rally, too. 'Cause people ought to see both sides of the story in order for them to see the whole picture."

Not all of the qualifications were based on concern for adequate information or people's feelings. For example, a tolerant male tenth grader linked the right to free speech to citizenship: "I mean you *have* to let them [the Nazis]. I mean, if they're citizens of the United States and stuff, it's their, I mean, they can . . . they have rights and stuff." Freedom of speech and assembly are not yet perceived by this student as fundamental human rights. Rather, his response is grounded in a legalistic orientation toward rights; citizenship provides a basis for freedom of speech and assembly.

The predominant qualification offered by the tolerant students, however, involved violence. For most (71 percent), the rally was to be supported as long as there was no violence. For example, a tolerant female tenth grader said, "I guess if they're [the Ku Klux Klan] gonna follow by the laws and it wouldn't be like violent, and it would be lawful, then they could do it. Cause they're people too. And they have the right to assemble, I guess." The perceived potential for violence has been identified as an important variable in predicting levels of tolerance (Gibson, 1987). On one hand, the students in the present study cannot be characterized as naive idealists since they recognized the possibility of violence. On the other hand, their decisions about whether or not to support a rally had to be made with imperfect information. The fact that they cannot accurately predict whether violence will occur did not appear to be problematic to them. One wonders if the students would have been willing to allow the rally if the group's past rallies had involved violence.

Only 44 percent of the intolerant students mentioned violence as a reason for disallowing the rally. This percentage is interesting when one considers that 71 percent of the tolerant students qualified their support for the rally in terms of violence. Other consequences appeared relevant for intolerant students: concern about the potential influence of the group on others (28 percent) and concern about the impact of the rally on the community (39 percent). For example, the following remarks are from two intolerant male tenth graders: "Because if they're [proabortionists] having rallies, then more people are gonna start looking at them and they . . . they're trying to get more people to be on their side about it. . . . You don't need anybody else killing babies." "Ah, I wouldn't let them [gay rights organization], I'd ask them not to do it. The town could end up getting the name as, you know, 'we go along with the view that the faggots' and that could in fact affect the business of the city." These students' concern for others and for their community contrasts with another student's, also an intolerant male tenth grader, more egocentric orientation: "I don't want to hear their [gay rights organization's] opinions or anything like that. I mean I know what they are about."

Although 33 percent of the intolerant students gave similar egocentric responses, none based his or her entire explanation solely on personal preferences. Most intolerant students focused their concerns on the negative consequences of the rally, whether the influence on others, violence, or harm to the community. Tolerant students were also likely to consider the potential negative consequences of the rally. As discussed in the next section, however, it is the *perceived likelihood* of these negative consequences that differentiates between tolerant and intolerant students.

Images of a Hypothetical Rally. The question "What do you suppose might happen if there were a rally in [name of the city]?" was asked to gain some understanding of students' conceptualizations of a hypothetical rally. Responses were coded in terms of two categories: actors (opposition groups and police) and actions (violent activities and nonviolent activities). Tolerant students were more likely to mention the police and nonviolent activities (for example, picketing or leafletting), and intolerant students were more likely to mention opposition groups and violence.

Only a small number of the total sample mentioned the police, and all of these students were in the tolerant group (24 percent). These students seemed to view the role of the police as provision of protection against violence. For example, a tolerant female tenth grader said, "I know some of them [antiabortionists] are violent; and if they are there, the police would be there, the police department of the city. I'm sure they would be there just to make sure everything's fine." Whether these students were naive or had simply had more positive experiences with authority is unknown. It is curious, however, that none of the intolerant students included the police in their hypothetical scenarios.

Nonviolent activities, such as speeches and marches, also appeared to be outside most of the students' repertoires with respect to their least-liked groups. The low frequency of mention of these activities may have been due to a lack of familiarity with rallies in general. Again, however, tolerant students (29 percent) were more likely to include such activities in their scenarios than were intolerant students (6 percent). Intolerant students were more likely than tolerant students to mention the presence of opposition at the rally (72 percent versus 43 percent, respectively) and the possibility of violence (83 percent versus 57 percent, respectively). It is important to note, moreover, that the opposition was vaguely generalized for most students. They spoke of "people who don't like the Ku Klux Klan" and "protesters" and "people against them." Only a few of the students (five tolerant and one intolerant) identified opposition groups (for example, blacks, Jews, and antiabortionists), and none cited specific organizations (for example, National Association for the Advancement of Colored People, Anti-Defamation League, and Right to Life). The omission of specific organizations underscores the degree to which political dissenters and dissent are viewed within simple cognitive structures.

The ways in which tolerant and intolerant students spoke about violence also differed. While tolerant students spoke of the *possibility* of violence, intolerant students were more likely to speak of the *probability* or *certainty* of violence. Compare the ways in which the first speaker (tolerant male tenth grader) and the second speaker (intolerant male tenth grader) considered violence: "Um, there would be probably a side that would . . . conflict like anti-Nazis, that would protect their, their rally . . . and there might be . . . I'm sure that there would be words mixed, but maybe a little bit of violence if it got out of hand." "There would be a lot of opposition [to the gay rights organization]. Not everybody is for that. Violence . . . I bet you . . . something would start up."

Linguists refer to modality as "the speaker's judgment of probability" (Halliday, 1982, p. 140). Of the thirty-six modal expressions used by tolerant students in response to the question about the hypothetical rally, 56 percent can be characterized as low-value ("I don't know, I'm not sure, I'm not certain") to moderately low-value modal expressions ("maybe, might, could possible, I guess, I think"). High-value ("I know, I'm certain, I'm sure") to moderately high-value modal expressions ("will, probably") accounted for the remaining 44 percent. The pattern is reversed for the intolerant students. Of the twenty-one modal expressions used, 24 percent indicated low to moderately low certainty; 76 percent were high-value to moderately high-value modal expressions. The modal expressions appeared to serve the function of justification, particularly for the intolerant students. If the likelihood of violence is quite high, then the action of prohibiting the rally is warranted. If the possibility of conflict is low, then support for the rally may be viewed as a reasonable decision.

Similarly, the intolerant students were less likely than the tolerant students to use the conditional mode ("if-then," "it depends") when describing the hypothetical rally (33 percent versus 6 percent, respectively). The following excerpt exemplifies the willingness of one tolerant student (a female eleventh grader) to entertain different possible outcomes: "Well . . . I don't know . . . just, it depends on what kind of, I mean, what kind of people . . . people they [antiabortionists] are. If they're violent, it could end up, you know, in a big mess, but um . . . I don't know, I would just find out the circumstances, where they were and what kinds of people are there, and like, if proabortionists were there, and stuff like that." Overall, tolerant students tended to approach the rally question with less certainty than their intolerant counterparts. They were more likely to engage in hypothetico-deductive thought processes; they acknowledged the lack of relevant information and considered the possibilities given certain circumstances.

Sources of Information. At the conclusion of the interview, students were asked how they had learned about their respective least-liked sociopolitical groups. The degree to which a group's historical and ideological contexts are discussed, distorted, or ignored may influence the way in which students construct their own images and interpretations of the group. For respondents in the present study, the tolerant students were more likely to cite sources such as newspapers (40 percent) and television news (55 percent) that provide opposing viewpoints of and in-depth information on outcast groups, compared with 29 percent of the intolerant students citing each of these sources. Family, friends, and school also provided tolerant students opportunities for discussing questions and concerns to a greater extent than was the case for intolerant students.

Perhaps the most important difference between the tolerant and intolerant students was the number of sources from which each group drew their information. Tolerant students were more likely than intolerant students to cite more than one source of information (75 percent versus 41 percent, respectively). By synthesizing data from multiple sources, the tolerant students may have felt more secure in their understanding of the group, its motives, and its potential threat.

Conclusion

Traditional survey items designed to measure political tolerance have generally failed to provide insights into individual perceptions of dissent and dissenters. More important, they have failed to reveal the complex issues associated with tolerance. The strategy employed in the study presented here allows us to identify extremely tolerant and intolerant students, and then to focus on some of the more complex dimensions of tolerance. The identified patterns of responses to interview questions suggest that tolerant and intolerant students have somewhat different conceptualizations of dissent and dissenters.

The tolerant students tended to display a broader knowledge and understanding of their least-liked groups; at the same time, they readily acknowledged their dislike for the groups' beliefs. They considered the potential negative consequences of dissent but let their belief in individual rights guide their judgments. Their support for freedom of assembly appeared fragile, however, and their rationales were as yet uncomplicated. The language of their tolerance was more tentative and less categorical.

Evaluations tended to play a more central role in the intolerant students' descriptions of their least-liked sociopolitical groups. Like the tolerant students, they considered the potential negative consequences of dissent; unlike their counterparts, they were more certain about effects. Issues of dissent seemed less problematic for these students. The language of their intolerance was more categorical and more definitive.

The tolerant and intolerant students shared a political discourse that was marked by generalities. They are, after all, citizens of a fundamentally stable democracy in which serious political conflict is not a matter that is often considered. Dissent and dissenters are removed from their daily lives. They also live in a society that has both tolerated and repressed political dissidents. Yet, there is little to compel these students to question or analyze such apparent inconsistencies.

Research on thinking specific to the political domain is fairly limited

(Torney-Purta, 1990). While many older adolescents appear cognitively capable of sophisticated reasoning about complex political issues, few actually demonstrate such abilities. The extent to which social, cultural, and historical contexts promote or inhibit the development of political reasoning has yet to be examined. Continued research in this area is needed to describe the relationships between political thinking and socialization processes.

References

Adams, G. R. "Identity and Political Socialization." In A. S. Waterman (ed.), Identity in Adolescence: Processes and Contents. New Directions for Child Development, no. 30. San Francisco: Jossey-Bass, 1985.

Adelson, J. "The Political Imagination of the Young Adolescent." Daedalus, 1971, 100, 1013–1050.

Avery, P. G. "Political Tolerance Among Adolescents." Theory and Research in Social Education, 1988, 16 (3), 183–201.

Corbett, M. Political Tolerance in America. White Plains, N.Y.: Longman, 1982.

Erikson, E. H. Identity, Youth, and Crisis. New York: Norton, 1968.

Gibson, J. L. "Homosexuals and the Ku Klux Klan: A Contextual Analysis of Political Tolerance." Western Political Quarterly, 1987, 40 (3), 427–448.

Gibson, J. L., and Bingham, R. D. "Elite Tolerance of Nazi Rights." American Politics Quarterly, 1983, 11 (4), 403–428.

Halliday, M.A.K. "The De-Automatization of Grammar: From Priestley's 'An Inspector Calls.'" In J. Answerdon (ed.), Linguistic Variation. Amsterdam, The Netherlands: John Benjamins, 1982.

Jones, R. S. "Democratic Values and Preadult Virtues: Tolerance, Knowledge, and Participation." Youth and Society, 1980, 12 (2), 189–220.

Kohlberg, L. "The Philosophy of Moral Development: Moral Stages and the Idea of Justice." In Essays on Moral Development. Vol. 1. New York: HarperCollins, 1981.

Marcus, G. E., Sullivan, J. L., and Theiss-Morse, B. "Political Tolerance and Threat: Affective and Cognitive Influences." Paper presented at the annual meeting of the Midwest Political Science Association, Chicago, April 5–8, 1990.

Miller, S. D., and Sears, D. O. "Stability and Change in Social Tolerance: A Test of the Persistence Hypothesis." American Journal of Political Science, 1986, 30 (1), 214–236.

Owen, D., and Dennis, J. "Preadult Development of Political Tolerance." Political Psychology, 1987, 8 (4), 847–851.

Patterson, J. W. "Moral Development and Political Thinking: The Case of Freedom of Speech." Western Political Quarterly, 1979, 32 (1), 7–20.

Sigel, R., and Hoskin, M. The Political Involvement of Adolescents. New Brunswick, N.J.: Rutgers University Press, 1981.

Sniderman, P. M., Tetlock, P. E., Glaser, J. M., Green, D. P., and Hout, M. "Principled Tolerance and the American Mass Public." British Journal of Political Science, 1989, 19, 25–45.

Stephan, W. "Stereotyping: Role of Ingroup-Outgroup Differences in Causal Attribution of Behavior." Journal of Social Psychology, 1977, 101, 255–266.

Stouffer, S. Communism, Conformity, and Civil Liberties. New York: Doubleday, 1955.

Sullivan, J. L., Piereson, J. E., and Marcus, G. E. Political Tolerance and American Democracy. Chicago: University of Chicago Press, 1982.

Torney-Purta, J. "Youth in Relation to Social Institutions." In S. Feldman and G. Elliott (eds.), At the Threshold: The Developing Adolescent. Cambridge, Mass.: Harvard University Press, 1990.

Zellman, G. L., and Sears, D. O. "Childhood Origins of Tolerance for Dissent." *Journal of Social Issues,* 1971, 27 (2), 109–137.

PATRICIA G. AVERY is assistant professor of Education at the University of Minnesota.

Socialization differs for political issues with personal relevance to U.S. adolescents.

The Personal and the Political in Reasoning and Action

Fayneese Miller

Over the last thirty years, researchers have been interested in the political socialization and development of adolescents. Interest was sparked by adolescents' involvement in national political concerns such as the Vietnam War and the civil rights movement during the 1960s. As those two events were moved off of the national agenda, adolescents' participation in political activities waned and the research on political socialization also decreased. A recent renewal of interest seems to have been precipitated by adult observations that adolescents are apathetic, politically alienated, or indifferent. Civic education programs, including community service programs, have emerged to counter these qualities in adolescents.

Within adolescents' everyday lives an important influence on their involvement is the perceived unfairness of political rules or policies, especially those judged to have a potential impact on psychological, social, or economic well-being (Sigel and Hoskin, 1981). Research in the area of procedural justice has found that people's responses to issues depends on whether or not they perceive the policies associated with the issue as appropriate and fair (Tyler, 1986). Further, during the economic crisis of the Great Depression in the 1930s, young people perceived the government and its policies as failures and responded by rejecting the political beliefs and party affiliations of their parents (Key, 1961).

In this chapter, I argue that adolescents respond to political events according to the perceived relevance to their own lives as well as to the prevailing conditions within society. In order to consider how the social and political context at all levels shapes responses of adolescents, a model of how adolescents think and reason about social issues is presented. It is proposed that how one thinks about political issues is influenced either by a perception that a particular issue has specific consequences for one's personal or economic well-being (instrumental belief) or by a socialized view of one's responsibility to the needs and concerns of others (symbolic belief). One purpose of this chapter is to examine the beliefs that underlie adolescents' attitudes toward social or political issues. A second purpose is to examine differences between reasoning about personally relevant issues and reasoning about issues that lack personal relevance.

Political Thinking and Activity of Adolescents

The prevailing view of adolescents throughout the 1980s was that they were politically apathetic and self-interested (Coffield and Buckalew, 1985; Miller, in press). A mere description of adolescents as apathetic, however, does not take into account their ability to reason about social and political events. It also fails to take into account adolescents' changing perspectives on rules and the relation of those rules to self and society. As Adelson (1971) proposed, adolescents develop an understanding of the role that they play in the political process and of the rules that govern that process. In other words, adolescents construct a "reality" concerning rules based on their ability to reason about intentions and on their understanding of collective norms.

Development of the ability to think through political issues is a precursor to political involvement. Although political involvement is usually defined as active participation in the political process (for example, voting, participating in peace demonstrations, and working on a political campaign), it is defined in this chapter as including indirect and direct participation in a wider range of political activities related to one's society or community. An example of indirect political involvement is the high school student who, when asked a series of questions about school restructuring and tracking, stated, "I see an elitist group emerging without sensitivities to lower classes" (Hakola, 1990, p. 212). This student was involved in thinking about the social and political structure, a form of indirect political involvement.

Most adolescents are capable of political thinking. Two different types of reasoning are important: (1) *Instrumental* reasoning involves the interpretation of issues or events based on perceived personal consequences. The focus is on expected outcomes of a particular issue or event for self or other individuals. The essential component of instrumental reasoning is consequences. If one perceives consequences for another, regardless of how close the self is to the other, then he or she is reasoning instrumentally. (2) *Symbolic* reasoning involves the interpretation of issues, events, or people based on symbols and prior social experiences. The focus is on the more abstract application of experiences as rules, values, or norms. The essential components of symbolic reasoning are principles, values, and social experiences that are at a distance from the individual and often associated with society as a whole.

Toward a Theory of Personal and Social Reasoning

Reasoning, according to Nickerson (1986, pp. 1-2), "involves production and evaluation of arguments, the making of inferences and the drawing of conclusions, the generation and the testing of hypotheses." It involves the use of cognitive and affective processes in the formation and evaluation of beliefs about and attitudes toward people or events. Social reasoning involves "reasoning about the relationship between individuals and between the individuals and society" (Weinreich-Haste, 1983, p. 87). This definition includes both cognitive and affective processes relating the individual to the polity, society, and the community.

The ultimate goal of a theory of personal and social reasoning is to understand the beliefs that underlie the ways that people think about and respond to other people or events. This developing theory does not assume that all behaviors or attitudes, especially those of adolescents, are under volitional control. This viewpoint contrasts with that of Ajzen and Fishbein (1980), who assume that people act in accordance with their intentions and that their behavior is not difficult to predict if behavioral intent is known. The problem with this model is that it overemphasizes behavioral intent and underemphasizes beliefs of which one may not be aware.

In the model proposed here of adolescent thought and reasoning, two basic components of reasoning are recognized, one personal and consequential in nature and the other social and value oriented. The personal factor is labeled instrumental reasoning. Instrumental beliefs focus on perceived personal consequences for self or other people, in other words, on what one believes will happen to self or other individuals within society if a particular issue or event is allowed to occur or continue (Miller and Abelson, 1985). The self-other distinction is important to the model because, according to self-perception research (see Prentice, 1990), we respond to and remember information differently when it has self-relevance. When information is personal and familiar, we tend to internalize it; but when information has no personal relevance and is unfamiliar, we tend to externalize it.

Symbolic beliefs, on the other hand, are general predispositions toward a target object, person, or event that do not have a personal connection. These predispositions are the result of early socialization practices that have their basis in societal or group-oriented norms and practices. Symbolic beliefs are value oriented and focus on a generalized rather than a particularized view of what one ought to do based on socialized beliefs about right versus wrong or fairness versus unfairness (Miller, 1986; Miller and Abelson, 1985).

Kinder and Sears (1985) have proposed that symbolic beliefs are based on the evaluation of group members as being something (egalitarianism), doing something (individualism), and having or not having something (post-materialism). Postmaterialism is evident in those who "express interest in a friendlier and less impersonal society, one that honors ideas more than money, that protects freedom of speech, and that encourages widespread participation in decision making" (Kinder and Sears, 1985, p. 676).

Let us contrast these two perspectives with respect to an issue. From a symbolic point of view, adolescents may be against a minimum-wage reduction for persons under eighteen years of age because they perceive the reduction as an indication that society devalues the contributions of adolescents (reasoning based on egalitarianism principle), does not recognize the individual diligence and discipline of adolescents (reasoning based on the individualism principle), and does not encourage adolescents to become a part of the decision-making process (reasoning based on the postmaterialism principle). These principles, which are based on values, serve as organizers of political thinking.

In contrast, from an instrumental perspective, the adolescent may be against a reduced minimum wage for adolescents under eighteen because it would mean that they or their peers would make less money. The focus of the instrumental response is on the consequences of a reduced minimum wage, not on the values that are associated with the wage proposal.

Although past research (Kelman, 1979) suggests that personal reasoning is self-oriented whereas social reasoning is other oriented, I propose that both instrumental and symbolic reasoning can be self- *and* other related. Consider the case of two secondary students who are asked about their beliefs and attitudes regarding cuts in educational loans and grants. How will they reason about the issue? What reasons will underlie their attitudes and beliefs? We need to know each student's content-specific social situation (in this case, prior experience with and current need for educational loans and grants) and their general attitudes and beliefs as expressed in their views on the educational "rights" of individuals. The theory of personal and social reasoning advanced here assumes that the relative importance of these two factors depends in part on the students' conceptualizations of the issue from a personal and a societal point of view. That is, the students' own experiences with loans and grants, and those of peers, will affect their positions on loans and grants. For example, an eleventh grader may respond to the issue somewhat differently from a ninth grader because educational loans and grants are a more salient issue.

Miller (1986), in a study of ninth and eleventh graders' political awareness and attitudes toward political issues such as federal budget cuts, examined the two categories of reasoning. The students were asked to respond to a series of belief and attitude statements about what a particular issue "would lead to" (consequence or instrumental statements) and what the issue "shows" (value or symbolic statements). In general, the students expressed opposition to federal budget cuts and gave reasons for their position such as the cuts "would lead to higher unemployment" (what would happen) and "show that the government doesn't care about needy people" (concern about the welfare of others). Both responses suggest indirect political involvement in the form of political thinking.

In an interview during a pretest session, one student's conceptualization of federal budget cuts was grounded in a concern about the effects on her family, families like hers, and her future educational aspirations. The student also called the cuts unfair and irresponsible. Most of the students interviewed were concerned about the consequences of different approaches to social issues, both for themselves and for other individuals.

Another example is reasoning about the drinking age. For example, a student who is under twenty-one may be in favor of the higher drinking age because raising the drinking age might lead to a reduction in the cost of their automobile insurance or that for other 16- to 25-year-olds (Miller, Stone, and Gainsburg, 1987). The emphasis for this student is on the consequences of a raised drinking age, both personally and for other adolescents. An example of symbolic reasoning is support of a raised drinking age based on the view that adolescents are not mature enough to handle alcohol.

The adolescent who is symbolically oriented in his or her thinking applies rules and values about the role of adolescents within society when reasoning about an issue. In other words, symbolic reasoning incorporates notions about the group and about individuals within the group. The self component in symbolic reasoning presupposes a view of self as attached to rather than separate from society. That is, notions about the self are associated with notions about other people and relationships to them.

In summary, both symbolic and instrumental reasoning emphasize the self and other as interactive. The difference between the two categories is that symbolic reasoning is value or principle oriented whereas instrumental reasoning is consequence oriented.

Figure 4.1 summarizes the personal and social reasoning discussion to this point. Past models of moral or social reasoning viewed self and other reasoning as mutually exclusive. A focus on the self or individual, in past models, was viewed as an indication of concrete thinking and therefore as less cognitively mature than a focus on the other, which was seen as incorporating abstract thinking. The proposed model, on the other hand, retains a focus on both self and other reasoning but does not assume that they are mutually exclusive; nor does it assume that concrete and abstract reasoning should be viewed exclusively from a developmental perspective. What the model does assume is that (1) both concrete and abstract reasoning are legitimate responses available to adolescents and (2) how an adolescent responds or reasons about an issue depends on the way in which he or she perceives the issue as related to the self and other people. Instrumental reasoning is more likely to take place when an issue

Figure 4.1. Comparison of Past Models of Moral Reasoning to Proposed Model of Personal and Social Reasoning

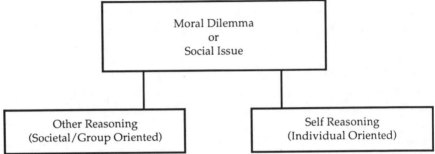

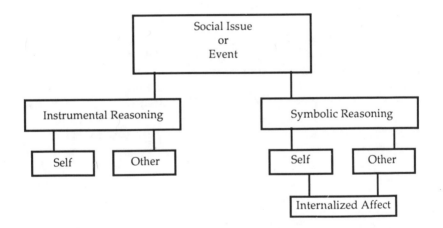

or a consequence of a political event is perceived as salient to the individual. Symbolic reasoning, in contrast, connects the individual and society and is dependent on both prior experience with social events and the internalization of affect associated with the socialization experience.

Other researchers have been interested in the role of symbolic beliefs or reasoning for understanding attitudes toward social or political issues (Kinder and Sears, 1985). Sears, Hensler, and Speers (1979) found that people tend to justify their opposition to busing with symbolic reasons that suggest either dissatisfaction with the federal government's civil rights policies (a procedural justice reasoning approach) or a belief in white superiority, rather than focus on such self-interested factors as a child in public school or busing in one's own community. Self-interest in the studies of Kinder and Sears and of Sears, Hensler, and Speers was an independent variable operationally defined by demographic variables such as having children in public schools. The proposed alternative shifts the focus from the assumption of social reasoning by virtue of certain demographic variables to the specific reasoning given by individuals for social or political beliefs (see Torney-Purta, 1989).

Symbolic and Instrumental Reasoning

In attempting to understand the reasons that underlie adolescents' social and political attitudes, I have focused on both symbolic and instrumental reasoning about several real-life issues. Students in the previously mentioned study on federal budget cuts were generally opposed to the cuts (Miller, 1986). Specifically, I found that minority high school students were concerned about the possible effects of federal budget cuts on other minority students as well as on their own participation in higher education. These students tended to use reasoning that was instrumental and consequence oriented.

Many of the students' reasons for their negative attitude toward federal budget cuts indicated their personal involvement with the issue and their identification with individuals or groups who might also be involved with the issue. Some student responses were also symbolically oriented: Federal budget cuts "show that the government doesn't care about needy people."

In another study (Miller, 1990a), I asked high school students about their attitudes toward a compulsory community service requirement for high school students. The purpose of the study was to compare how high school students reason about issues that have great personal relevance with how they reason about issues that have less personal relevance. Each student was administered a questionnaire that contained a fictitious summary (message statement) of a proposal that was supposedly before the legislature in either a northern or a southern state. The message stated that the state legislature was considering a proposal that would require all high school students to complete fifty hours of community service before receiving their high school diplomas. After reading the message statement, the students were asked to respond to a series of attitude and belief statements about the proposal and to list their thoughts (cognitive listing). The students' level of involvement with the issue (high or low) was defined by whether their home state was in the region (north or south) referred to in the message.

Students in the low-involvement condition gave more instrumental responses to the question "How might we encourage high school students to become involved in community service activities?'" than did students in the high-involvement condition, who gave more symbolic responses. Although this finding might seem to contradict the earlier statement that instrumental reasoning relates to perceived salience, it does not. As previously mentioned, instrumental reasoning involves a focus on perceived consequences for other people as well as the self. It appears that the low-involvement students identified with the plight of the high-involvement students, which made the issue more salient to them. Since the students did not perceive themselves as directly affected by the proposal, the link between the self and the community had not been formed. For example, some of the instrumental responses that low-involvement students gave were "praise students for their involvement" or "give students credit for their involvement." On the other hand, high-involvement students tended to give symbolic responses such as "encourage greater identification with one's community" and "increase students' pride in their communities or other students." Females gave significantly more symbolic reasoning responses (for example, "helping others helps the self," "many people need help—it's our duty to help other people," and "it is good or right to do for others") than did males, who gave more instrumental responses (for example, "offer extra credit," "give money for students' services," and "give public recognition").

There were also differences by age. The reasons that seniors gave for being opposed to the proposal were more often of the procedural justice type (for example, "the proposal violates my right to freedom of choice and is being instituted without input from those it will affect"); whereas the freshmen tended to oppose the proposal because of a lack of perceived tangible rewards, such as money and course credit, for participation. In contrast to the subjects in Tyler's (1986) study, these subjects focused on the fairness of the policies for all people (egalitarian value) and on what the policies meant in terms of distribution of outcomes or rewards (individualism value), rather than on simply the policies and consequences associated with implementation of a community service proposal. The subjects' responses suggest a quite complex and organized system of reasoning (see Miller, 1990a).

In another study of the way in which adolescents organize their reasoning about social and political issues (Miller, 1990b), tenth- through twelfth-grade students were asked about their attitudes and beliefs on homelessness (a nonpersonal issue) and on a clean school (a personal issue). The students were presented with a videotaped message about each issue. The presenter of the message was either an adolescent or an adult. The homelessness message was about the educational plight of homeless children. The clean school message was about a school with a dirty cafeteria, classrooms, and hallways. The students were asked to give reasons for their attitudes on each issue.

Students who received the message about a clean school from the adolescent presenter gave reasons for their attitudes such as it "would decrease the amount of work the janitors have to do and we do pay them to clean up after students," "would lead to mockery of those students who get involved by those who don't," and "would decrease the amount of time we have to do other things." These students' responses toward the clean school issue tended to be primarily instrumental or consequence oriented.

In contrast, the students who received the message about a clean school from the adult presenter tended to give more symbolic responses, such as keeping one's school clean "shows that students care about their school and each other," "shows that students have school pride," or "the clean school issue shows that society needs to be reformed." The association of the message with an adult rather than a peer seemed to generate more abstract and symbolic value-oriented reasoning.

Students who received the message about homelessness gave more symbolic than instrumental responses, overall. The students appeared to be unfamiliar with the issue of homeless children and viewed it as a societal rather than a personally relevant problem. The students therefore focused more on the processes associated with homelessness (procedural justice approach) than on the outcomes of homelessness. Some of the student responses were that "students need to be taught how to respond to other people's problems," "students would be more knowledgeable about these kinds of issues if parents and teachers stopped treating them like children," "students want to help but feel as though we don't know how to help," and "nobody has faith or trusts youth today, give us a chance, we can make a difference." The responses appeared to be based on a belief that students should be given the opportunity to help other people.

The findings of the research presented in this section suggest that social and political reasoning includes both societal and individual components organized around either instrumental or symbolic thinking. The findings suggest that the ways in which adolescents reason about social issues depend on their perceptions of their relationships to other individuals and to society.

Conclusion

It has been argued in this chapter that adolescents respond to political events according to the perceived relevance of the events to their own lives, to the lives of other individuals, and to the prevailing social conditions within society. There are clearly "developmental" components in adolescents' reasoning in that older adolescents are generally more able to use and understand abstract concepts. However, a problem with traditional developmental models is the tendency to equate "concrete" with "individual-centered" reasoning and "abstract" with "society-centered" reasoning. The argument of this chapter is that a focus on the consequences for individuals (and the self) or a focus on society and principles may be context-specific and depend on how the respondent perceives the situation. Thus, a more representative view of the ways in which adolescents think through and reason about political issues may be achieved by focusing on the ways in which adolescents organize their reasoning.

Two categories of reasoning are proposed in this chapter: instrumental and symbolic. Instrumental reasoning, which is consequence oriented, is based on the belief that a political issue has consequences for one's personal well-being. Symbolic reasoning, on the other hand, is principle or value oriented and involves the application of values, norms, or rules to political issues. An individual interprets and responds to political issues according to his or her personal and social relationships to self and other individuals.

Research on the notion that reasoning is both instrumentally and symbolically constructed is not new. Researchers in the areas of symbolic racism, procedural justice, moral reasoning, and social reasoning have discussed the role of social norms and values (societal reasoning) in the reasoning process. However, they have dealt with either the acquisition of internalized belief structures or the development of social-cognitive or reasoning structures. I propose that by joining the two areas of research, a better understanding of the role of society, social institutions, and social or political issues in evoking social reasoning can be achieved.

References

Adelson, J. "The Political Imagination of the Young Adolescent." *Daedalus*, 1971, *100*, 1013–1050.

Ajzen, I., and Fishbein, M. *Understanding Attitudes and Predicting Social Behavior*. Englewood Cliffs, N.J.: Prentice Hall, 1980.

Coffield, K. E., and Buckalew, L. W. "University Student Apathy: Sex, Race, and Academic Class Variables." *Psychological Record*, 1985, *35*, 459–463.

Hakola, B. "As Top High School Students Tackle Nation's Problems, They Express Isolation from Crisis in Education." *Education USA*, 1990, *32*, 212.

Kelman, H. C. "The Role of Action in Attitude Change." In H. E. Howe and M. M. Page (eds.), Nebraska Symposium on Motivation: *Beliefs, Attitudes, and Values*. Vol. 27. Lincoln: University of Nebraska Press, 1979.

Key, V. O. *Public Opinion and American Democracy*. New York: Knopf, 1961.

Kinder, D. R., and Sears, D. O. "Public Opinion and Political Actions." In G. Lindzey and E. Aronson (eds.), *The Handbook of Social Psychology*. Vol. 2. New York: Erlbaum, 1985.

Miller, F. S. "Symbolic Versus Instrumental Beliefs: An Analysis of Black and White High School Students' Attitudes Toward Policy Issues." In H. P. McAdoo (ed.), *Proceedings of the Ninth Conference on Empirical Research in Black Psychology*. Rockville, Md.: National Institute of Mental Health, 1986.

Miller, F. S. "Gender Differences in Adolescents' Attitudes Toward Compulsory Community Service." Unpublished manuscript, Brown University, 1990a.

Miller, F. S. "Towards an Understanding of Adolescents' Reasoning About Personal and Societal Issues." Unpublished manuscript, Brown University, 1990b.

Miller, F. S., and Abelson, R. P. "Beliefs and Values as Determinants of Attitudes Toward

Policy Issues." Paper presented at the 85th annual meeting of the American Psychological Association, Los Angeles, August 1985.

Miller, F. S., Stone, E., and Gainsburg, J. "Symbolic Versus Instrumental Arguments: Its Effects on Information Processing." Paper presented at the 58th annual meeting of the Eastern Psychological Association, Arlington, Virginia, March 1987.

Nickerson, R. S. Reflections on Reasoning. Hillsdale, N.J.: Erlbaum, 1986.

Prentice, D. A. "Familiarity and Differences in Self- and Other-Representations." Journal of Personality and Social Psychology, 1990, 59, 369-383.

Sears, D. O., Hensler, C. P., and Speers, L. K. "Whites' Opposition to 'Busing': Self-Interest or Symbolic Racism?" American Political Science Review, 1979, 73, 369-384.

Sigel, R., and Hoskin, M. The Political Involvement of Adolescents. New Brunswick, N.J.: Rutgers University Press, 1981.

Torney-Purta, J. "Political Cognition and Its Restructuring in Young People." Human Development, 1989, 32, 14-23.

Tyler, T. R. "The Psychology of Leadership Evaluation." In H. W. Bierhoff, R. L. Cohen, and J. Greenberg (eds.), Justice in Social Relations. New York: Plenum, 1986.

Weinreich-Haste, H. "Social and Moral Cognition." In H. Weinreich-Haste and D. Locke (eds.), Morality in the Making. New York: Wiley, 1983.

FAYNEESE MILLER is associate professor of education and child study at Brown University.

Socialization entails insight into the nature of institutional authority among Scottish and French children.

Childhood Origins of Beliefs About Institutional Authority

Nicholas Emler

The evolution of the contemporary nation state has depended on the parallel evolution of forms of social coordination and control that extend beyond face-to-face relations among people who are related by blood, marriage, or personal acquaintance. The classic analysis of these evolutions and of the formal elements in social relationships was provided by Max Weber (1947). For Weber, the key process was the "bureaucratization" of relationships. Weber's point was that this process is a peculiarly modern experience; only from the nineteenth century onward have bureaucracies pervaded so many areas of life. This transformation in the relationship between individual and society rendered accommodation to bureaucracy and its requirements central to the process of political socialization in modern times.

Weber argued that the bureaucracy differs from other kinds of social organization, notably those based on ties of personal loyalty and those based on respect for custom and tradition, in the nature of the authority relations that underpin it, relations that he characterized as "legal-rational." His analysis of this form of authority emphasizes the following four features: (1) All positions of formal authority exist within a rationally organized hierarchy— an institution or organization—and have no legitimacy except in terms of their positions in this system. (2) Each position always has specific, explicit, and formally defined and limited spheres of jurisdiction. (3) Holders of this authority can only legitimately exercise it in accordance with formally defined, impersonal, and impartial criteria, and not in the service of personal

The original research described in this chapter was supported by ESRC Grant No. I 10230013 and CNRS Grant No. 95 5118.

interests. (4) Office holders have formally defined duties and obligations that are likewise distinct from their personal inclinations.

A system of government that rests on bureaucratic administration requires, if Weber is correct, a particular combination of understandings and attitudes. Thus, if as citizens we obey the instructions of police officers or other agents of the state, it is not because of any personal relationship between ourselves and the individual occupants of these positions. Nor is it because they personally have the capacity to reward or punish. Ideally, it is because we judge that they are formally authorized to issue these instructions and directives, and we are therefore formally obliged to comply. In return, we expect that state officials will act only within the limits of their formally defined authority, and that they will act entirely impartially, without any intrusion of personal feeling into their decisions. Likewise, we should ideally comply with the requirements of the law insofar as we regard legal requirements as the products of legitimate and constitutional process.

This complex of social understandings and attitudes implies that two conditions must be fulfilled among the adult members of the population. First, they must have some understanding of the principles of the social system. Second, they need to conclude that others, and in particular those acting in an official capacity, are indeed acting in accordance with these principles. Research indicates that when this second condition is not fulfilled, people are less likely to comply with the law or to obey officials of the state. Tyler (1990) concluded that compliance with the law is closely linked to perceptions that procedures for its administration and enforcement are executed impartially. Similarly, Reicher and Emler (1985) found a strong association among adolescents between behavioral defiance of the law and institutional authority, on the one hand, and beliefs that the legal system is biased and partial, on the other.

So what determines the degree to which these two conditions are met, namely, beliefs about the nature of bureaucracy and legal-rational authority, and beliefs that the representatives of the state are acting according to their requirements? This chapter considers the developmental dimension underlying these beliefs.

Cognitive Development

From the perspective of traditional cognitive developmental theory, the relationship between individual and formal authority can be analyzed in terms of degree of understanding. Bureaucracies can be regarded as objective features of the social landscape, much like banks or institutions of buying and selling (see Berti and Bombi, 1988); they are systems of relationships with an objective structure that can be analyzed and understood more or less adequately.

The social relationships that define bureaucracies have a structure that can be represented in terms of various logical relations. Thus, the ideas of a hierarchy of authority and of rationally distributed spheres of jurisdiction imply such concepts as seriation, class inclusion, and reciprocity. The logical complexity of bureaucracies is such that one might expect young children to have at best only a vague appreciation of their operation. Up to the present, however, there has been little research into the capacity of children at different ages or developmental levels to represent bureaucracy and its principles of operation.

Bureaucracies entail moral as well as objective or logical relations. Weber's analysis concerns how relationships are organized and the limits to the powers of office holders, but it also refers to beliefs about how people *ought* to behave in bureaucratic roles. So what clues might we discover in the moral development literature about the development of insight into the character and legitimacy of formal authority?

Kohlberg's (1984) stage-developmental theory provides one important source of clues. Of the five developmental stages that Kohlberg defined in detail, the fourth appears to mark the first emergence of a clear grasp of the moral legitimacy of formal authority. Authority at all stages prior to Stage 4 is interpreted in personal or interpersonal terms, by reference to individual interests, personal agreements and commitments, and personal relationships. At the fourth or "social systems" stage, there is recognition of the social structure that lies behind and legitimates rules and duties. In deciding what is right, one takes the detached perspective of a member of the social system, a citizen, rather than that of any of the concrete individuals involved in any moral dispute. Issues of reward and punishment are regarded in impersonal and impartial terms. Equality is the uniform and regular administration of the law according to objective and impersonal standards. The obligation to comply with the law is distinguished from the moral requirements of the more informal standards contained in shared norms and stereotypes.

The fifth stage appears to embrace a more sophisticated analysis of formal authority and a fuller appreciation of its limitations. Data collected by Kohlberg and others (see Snarey, 1985) indicate that Stage 4 moral reasoning is common among adults, but only those who inhabit industrialized, urbanized societies. It is rather less common among the adult members of other societies. If we assume that legal-rational authority is primarily a feature of the former kind of society, then this pattern of differences is much as we might expect.

However, Kohlberg's data also indicate that Stage 4 reasoning is very uncommon among people younger than sixteen, even among the relatively well-educated, socially advantaged members of industrialized societies. Is it indeed the case that there is no real understanding of the nature of formal authority prior to this age? Research on insight into organizational roles suggests otherwise. Two lines of work deserve our particular attention, relating to the formal elements in organizational roles and to the limits of authority.

Formal-Personal Distinction. Two programs of research, by Adelson (1971) and by Furth (1978), into children's beliefs about organizational roles have addressed this distinction. Furth's study of five- to eleven-year-olds' understanding of occupational or, as Furth described them, "societal" roles suggests that children do not recognize the formal and impersonal elements in role relations until they reach adolescence. They are not initially able to recognize that relations between people can be regulated by factors beyond personal inclinations or preferences. "Societal decisions are thought to emanate from the free will of a particular person" (Furth, 1978, p. 251). In other words, the distinction between the formal and the personal is a cognitively complex notion that appears relatively late in childhood. This conclusion is supported by Adelson's work, which indicates that eleven- and even thirteen-year-olds have little if any understanding of formal, institutionally based authority and are still inclined to confuse official obligations with personal wishes.

Limits of Authority. Several studies have revealed that even quite young children perceive that authority has limits (Damon, 1977; Turiel, 1983; Tisak, 1986; Piaget, 1932). These studies demonstrate children's beliefs that any person's authority is limited to what is also morally justifiable. In effect, there are perceived limitations on the exercise of all authority; no person can legitimately instruct another to do something that violates basic moral requirements. Parents cannot legitimately order children to steal, or lie, or physically assault innocent victims. There are various points here that we should notice. First, in most of these studies, no age trend was observed. Even the youngest children who were questioned, typically six-year-olds, appeared to understand that such limits exist. The one exception is Piaget's (1932) unreplicated finding that young children accepted the moral infallibility of people in authority, particularly parents, whereas older children argued that even the orders of parents were open to dispute if they conflicted with, for example, requirements of equal treatment. This finding raises the interesting possibility that the development of insight into authority is a progressive sorting out of just how much discretion people in authority have.

However, beliefs about the moral propriety of the exercise of authority are also likely to be linked to beliefs about the motivations of authority figures. We know from other research that young children regard authority figures as benevolently intentioned and only gradually does this belief give way to a more dispassionate and sometimes cynical view of people in authority. It may be that this developmental trend reflects a gradual differentiation between the office holder and the office, and a growing recognition of the human vulnerability of office holders and, consequently, of the need to control and limit their power.

A second point is that, in practice, the moral limits of authority are often ambiguous. In organizational contexts, the issue of just where those limits lie is a matter for continual negotiation between people in authority and those over whom they seek to exercise it.

Weber, however, was concerned not just with the moral limits of authority but with the rational organization of those limits. He argued that bureaucratic organization means different individuals having different kinds and spheres of authority. It is not just that parents can legitimately demand of their children only certain things; they can also demand different kinds of things from, for example, teachers or police officers. And, of course, authority is hierarchically ordered. Parents are subject to the authority of others whose formal powers are more extensive than their own.

The research cited above tells us little about these issues of ambiguity and negotiation, jurisdiction and hierarchy. However, two studies appear to describe childhood insights that are closer to Weber's concept of bureaucratic or legal-rational authority. Damon (1977), for instance, uses the example of a football team captain exceeding the authority of his particular position. In a study by Laupa and Turiel (1986), children distinguished between orders given by someone authorized to do so from orders given by people lacking proper authority.

Social Construction of Understanding and Belief

The classic cognitive developmental interpretation of the *process* of development has been that individual children progressively construct their own understandings of the social world (see Haste and Torney-Purta, this volume). Analysis of the development of social knowledge and moral judgment has rested on a general theory of the process of developmental change. Given that the general principles of change have been assumed to apply to all domains of knowledge, researchers have more often directed their attention to the "what" than to the "how" of development, occasionally making reference to instances that seem to demonstrate the process of spontaneous individual discovery and reconstruction at work (for example, Furth, 1978).

Strict individual constructivism, however, provides a limited explanation of the processes by which children acquire beliefs about formal organization and formal authority, and probably a limited account of many other domains of knowledge as well (Emler, 1987). Here, I briefly discuss the nature of those limits and then describe the findings from research I have conducted with colleagues in France (Emler, Ohana, and Moscovici, 1987; Emler, Ohana, and Dickinson, 1990).

First, cognitive developmental theory has assumed that human society in its fundamentals is always and everywhere the same. Bureaucracy is not a human universal but a historically and culturally relative social form. Experience of bureaucracy and the need to make some sense of it thus only arise for individuals inhabiting particular kinds of cultures. This directs our attention to the availability of experience of bureaucracy and formal authority, and to the consequences of this availability for the development of relevant beliefs.

Second, cognitive developmental theory implies that experience of the social environment is relatively direct and unproblematic. In contrast, I argue that every child, like every adult, is immersed not just in his or her own experiences but also in the accounts, explanations, and interpretations of the social world that circulate in any human community. Thus, children acquire knowledge of the social environment itself and also of these various "social representations" of that environment.

Third, cognitive developmental theory has traditionally assumed that individuals construct their own knowledge of the world. The fact that they construct the same beliefs about this world as other individuals does not imply the play of any social influence on development. Just as any two observers, armed only with their own personal observations of the world, should, given sufficient experience, arrive independently at the principles of buoyancy and of proportionality in a balance (Inhelder and Piaget, 1958), so also should they come to the same conclusions about the principles of formal organization. I suggest it is more probable that consensus about the social world, insofar as it exists, is the product of social interaction and social influence. Children not only are presented with all kinds of prepackaged and preexplained experience by the societies that they inhabit, but their own sense-making activity is always likely to be a social process, one in which they share and discuss experiences with others and come to conclusions that are constructed collectively, something more frequently recognized in cognitive developmental research than in statements of theory.

The implications of the foregoing are that (1) we should examine the content as well as the structure of social knowledge, (2) we should consider the availability of relevant experience and explanations, (3) we should be alert to the probability that different children are exposed to different experiences and accounts, by virtue of the kind of society that they inhabit and the respective positions of their immediate communities within that society, and (4) the particularities of shared experiences are reflected in shared beliefs.

Children's Beliefs About Organizational Roles

My own research has been guided by these various expectations. My colleagues and I anticipated that children's views about organizational roles and formal authority would vary as a function not only of age but also of culture, and of their own positions in the class-structure of society. As a cultural invention, the nature and extent of the development of bureaucracy and the image that it has within a society vary. The process of growing up within a particular social class exposes the child to the political perspectives of that class, including perspectives on the exercise of bureaucratic power in society.

We also assumed that the most important source of experience of formal organization in childhood is the school. It provides most children with their first direct and extended experience of a bureaucratic organization (Dreeban, 1968). Hence, it is with respect to this institution that children will first demonstrate any clear understanding of the nature of bureaucracy and of legal-rational authority. Cullen (1987) has provided some evidence for this prediction. The eight- and eleven-year-olds in her study were better than the five-year-olds at recognizing legitimate authority figures in a structured authority situation and at giving justifications for their authority, but the five-year-olds demonstrated more insight when the context given was the school. Cullen concluded that even in their first year at school, children are able to establish realistic and functional notions of authority.

Finally, if schools present children with experience of a bureaucratically organized institution, they can also present this experience in very different ways. Thus, the kind of school attended may also influence children's developing understanding.

Our studies have compared children from cultures that are politically, economically, and technologically similar within Britain and France. The children in the first study (Emler, Ohana, and Moscovici, 1987), 123 from the east of Scotland and 63 from the Paris region of France, were aged seven to eleven years. They were either from middle- or working-class backgrounds. The research was based on interviews organized around the description of various incidents within a school setting. The first of these dealt with the assessment of pupil performance, the second with the distribution of help by a teacher to different pupils in the class, and the third with the enforcement of school rules. The intention was to cover major forms of transactions that might occur between a teacher in his or her organizational role and children in their role as pupils. The questions elicited children's beliefs and understanding about such issues as the hierarchical nature of authority in the school, the requirements of impartiality, and the boundaries to teachers' formal authority.

Answers to several questions hint at a more sophisticated interpretation of organizational roles in this age group than is suggested in previous research. By eleven years of age, almost all of the children recognized that there is a hierarchy of authority in the school and that teachers are in their turn subject to the authority of persons, such as school principals or governments, above them in this hierarchy. Consider the following remarks of an eleven-year-old girl:

JACQUI: They [teachers] could make classroom rules but they would not be able to make whole school rules.

INTERVIEWER: Who can make school rules?

JACQUI: Headmaster.

INTERVIEWER: Could he make a rule to say children should come to school on Saturdays?

JACQUI: No, that would be the government.

Piaget's (1932) research drew attention to children's developing beliefs about the alterability of social rules. But Piaget studied children's insights about rules in the special context of children's games. Rather different conditions apply to the alterability of organizational rules, and our research revealed another kind of age trend here. Older children were more likely to believe that teachers do not have the authority to alter any rule at will. They appeared to recognize that teachers are themselves bound by regulations and have limited rule-making powers.

Most of the children in our sample also believed that it is wrong for teachers to allow their personal preferences to influence decisions about which pupils they would and would not help. For example, Clare, an eleven-year-old, said, "That wouldn't be a proper teacher. She wouldn't . . . I don't think she would be allowed to stay at school if she did that. Teachers have to be just, and all the children in the class may need as much help and she wouldn't be allowed to do that." In these cases, the middle-class and the French children were more likely to show these insights than were the working-class and the Scottish children.

Recognition of formal limits to the jurisdiction of teachers' authority was less clear-cut, and there was little discernible age trend here, perhaps because there actually is considerable ambiguity about jurisdiction. Children could agree that teachers had a right to tell them what work to do in the classroom but not, except in the case of some of the youngest children, what time they should go to bed: "This is absolutely ridiculous," protested one eleven-year-old!

In some areas of judgment, there were clear variations that did not fall on a single developmental dimension. Scottish and French children had different views about the obligations of office holders. The former claimed that teachers were bound to enforce regulations, whatever their personal feelings about the fairness of these regulations. This belief was more widespread among the middle-class children and among the older children, and it is tempting therefore to see this finding as evidence of a growing awareness of objective constraints on officials. In contrast, however, almost all of the French children argued the teacher should do what was fair, whatever the regulation required, although they were no less likely than their Scottish counterparts to anticipate that teachers would be sanctioned in some way if they ignored particular regulations. Likewise, Scottish children believed that it was appropriate for teachers to justify their actions by invoking the governing regulations. For example, Brian, eleven years old, was asked about a teacher who refuses to allow a small boy to borrow a book from the library and who cites the rule against it as her reason. Brian answered, "It is quite a good reason because it means it is not that she doesn't want to, it is the same for everyone." French children more often rejected this idea; in general, they seemed more "sophisticated" about bureaucracy, recognizing its features earlier and also being more critical of it.

It is the case, nonetheless, that between six and ten years of age, awareness of the organizational context is largely intuitive. Children seldom explicitly spell out a rationale for the actions of teachers in terms of their organizational role and its formal requirements. Turiel (1983) has said that the domain of personal preference is recognized, even by young children, as distinct from domains of conventional obligations and moral requirements. However, in a second study of 150 six-, eight-, and ten-year-olds in Britain and France, we found that children in this age range often still fail to see a difference between action that is formally required by a role and action that is a matter of personal preference. These children were asked about a teacher who said that she would teach reading only to pupils she liked and a skater on a pond who told children watching that he would show only those he liked how to skate. We asked whether it was right for each of these people to make this condition, and whether there was any difference between them. Most children thought that the teacher was wrong to deny help to pupils she did not like, but they made the same judgment about the skater. If they argued that there was a difference between the two cases, they were more likely to mention the nature of the activity (for example, "reading is more important than skating") than differences in the obligations of teachers and private citizens. The following excerpt from a ten-year-old's interview is one of the few examples of a child who explicitly mentioned this difference.

INTERVIEWER: Was it okay for the teacher to say that?
MARTHA: No.
INTERVIEWER: Why?
MARTHA: Because the teacher's been told to do that and she's meant to teach the children.
INTERVIEWER: Was it okay for the skater to say that?
MARTHA: Yes, it is fair because he can choose whatever he likes to do.
INTERVIEWER: Is there a difference?
MARTHA: Difference.
INTERVIEWER: Why?
MARTHA: The teacher has been taught to teach the children to learn to read and write and whereas the man is doing his own thing, what he wants to do.
　　On the other hand, there is Kate, also age ten, who initially seems to

spell out the impersonal and impartial character of a teacher's obligations but then argues that the other case is the same.

INTERVIEWER: Was it okay for the teacher to say that?
KATE: No.
INTERVIEWER: Why?
KATE: Well it's just that if you're going to be a teacher, you should teach all children. It's not whether you like them or not.
INTERVIEWER: Was it okay for the skater to say that?
KATE: No.
INTERVIEWER: Why?
KATE: Well it's the same as the teacher, because he shouldn't say no because he doesn't like them.
INTERVIEWER: Is there a difference?
KATE: There's not really a difference.
INTERVIEWER: Why not?
KATE: Because it's the same thing happening with both the pictures because they're both saying no because they don't like the children.

Daniel, age eight, starts off without any clear statement of role obligations and then begins to argue for a difference.

INTERVIEWER: Is it okay for the teacher to say that?
DANIEL: No.
INTERVIEWER: Why?
DANIEL: Because she might like them but it's not really fair on the others, because they won't learn to read very well.
INTERVIEWER: Is it okay for the skater to say that?
DANIEL: It might be, sort of.
INTERVIEWER: Is there a difference?
DANIEL: I think so.
INTERVIEWER: Why?
DANIEL: For one thing, they're different people altogether and they're not sort of the same, they're not the same place. And the teacher's meant to be helping other children where the man doesn't really have to.
INTERVIEWER: Which is worst?
DANIEL: I think the teacher's being more unfair.
INTERVIEWER: Why?
DANIEL: She's saying only what she, only people she likes are going to do it and she's meant to help all the others.

When we asked whether anyone else had the right to tell the teacher or the skater to help all of the children learn, the children whom we questioned were much more likely to see a difference, and some were explicit about the reason for this difference, as in the following response from James, age six.

INTERVIEWER: Does anyone have the right to tell the teacher to do that?
JAMES: Yes.
INTERVIEWER: Who?
JAMES: The head teacher.
INTERVIEWER: Does anyone have the right to tell the skater to do that?
JAMES: No.
INTERVIEWER: Why not?
JAMES: Because he does not work for the school and he does not know them.

On the other hand, we found children who argued that parents had the same kind of authority over skaters in the park as did headmasters and headmistresses over teachers.

We have also begun to examine the different representations of social organization and formal authority that may arise in traditionally organized schools versus "experimental" schools. Ohana (1987) compared children attending experimental schools in the Paris region with children attending more traditional schools in the area. Children in the traditional schools represented the schools' functioning around a rigid hierarchy. In the conceptualization of a ten-year-old at the bottom is the child, followed by the teacher, then the head teacher "who governs the school," and then the inspector, "the director who is above the head mistress." Social relations are based on obedience to formal or statutory authority. In the words of an eleven-year-old, "If the mistress says you must do it, you must do it." Children also asserted the necessity of obeying rules, as in the following examples from an eight-year-old and a ten-year-old, respectively: "You cannot disobey the rules, . . . you don't have the right." "If that is the rule, it's obvious you can't do anything else." The children also characterized teacher-pupil relations in authoritarian terms, as in the following remarks of an eight-year-old and an eleven-year-old, respectively: "A child cannot contradict the mistress, in relation to him she is always right." "The mistress is in charge; the children can't tell her who she should help most, the mistress has the right to do what she wants."

Children in the experimental schools represented authority in terms of a hierarchical network with several levels, involving dependence and the necessity of obedience by those at the bottom in relation to those higher up. However, the children also represented a capacity to bring pressure to bear and to exert influence in an upward direction. Thus, when questioned about a situation in which a teacher refuses to let a child take a book from the school library, an eight-year-old answered, "If he really wants the book, the mistress will give it to him and if not he can go and complain to the head teacher if he wants, he can go and tell his parents who would go and complain to the head."

Social relations at the experimental schools appeared to be organized in terms of respect for authority, as indicated in the following remarks of a ten-year-old: "The mistress must respect the law of the school; we respect it. We don't have the right to leave the school and not before the bell rings at 4:30. We respect it . . . because something might happen to us. . . . Those who don't respect it are dressed down because we don't want it [the school] to be finished, or else the school would have to pay big fines."

These children also represented the functioning of the school and the transactions taking place within it as founded on a social consensus achieved through discussion and negotiation. Thus, an eight-year-old child said, "The head, when he has something to say, it's necessary that everyone agrees because if he is the only person in the school who agrees, it wouldn't work." A ten-year-old child represented resolution of conflicts in terms of discussion: "If we don't share this opinion at all, we talk about it." And another ten-year-old said, "What's good here is that the teachers, before deciding, always ask the children's advice and if we are against it we try to discuss it."

Among these children, the model of decision making in the school and in the classroom was the majority vote. The following remarks are from a nine-year-old and an eleven-year-old, respectively: "In the class we all take the decisions together; we suggest something and then we see what is the best, and then we vote." "It's always the majority that counts, it's like when one is president, . . . it's true that there are very [weak] majorities, ten against nine; well, then it is necessary to discuss and take the nine into consideration."

Conclusion

Perhaps the most important lesson to be drawn here is that by the end of their elementary education, children have extensive and well-developed representations of institutional authority, and it is largely the experience of formal education that has provided the context for these developments. A second conclusion is that there are variations in the representations that emerge over this period of life, reflecting the influences of class, culture, and type of formal education. Future research should address the extent of these group differences and the social processes that underlie them, as well as the manner in which understandings of authority developed in childhood feed into the more overtly political beliefs and attitudes of adolescence and adulthood.

Work on the manner in which children accommodate to this central feature of contemporary social life is only beginning. There is much more to be discovered about the detail of children's understandings of formal authority and the social structures that underpin it.

References

Adelson, J. "The Political Imagination of the Young Adolescent." *Daedalus*, 1971, *100*, 1013–1050.

Berti, A. E., and Bombi, A. S. *The Child's Construction of Economics*. Cambridge, England: Cambridge University Press, 1988.

Cullen, J. L. "Relating to Authority in the Elementary School Years." *Child Study Journal*, 1987, *17*, 227–238.

Damon, W. *The Social World of the Child*. San Francisco: Jossey-Bass, 1977.

Dreeban, R. *On What Is Learned in School*. Reading, Mass.: Addison-Wesley, 1968.

Emler, N. "Moral Development from the Perspective of Social Representations." *Journal of the Theory of Social Behaviour*, 1987, *17*, 371–388.

Emler, N., Ohana, J., and Dickinson, J. "Children's Representations of Social Relations." In G. Duveen and B. Lloyd (eds.), *Social Representations and the Development of Knowledge*. Cambridge, England: Cambridge University Press, 1990.

Emler, N., Ohana, J., and Moscovici, S. "Children's Beliefs About Institutional Roles: A Cross-National Study of Representations of the Teacher's Role." *British Journal of Educational Psychology*, 1987, *57*, 26–37.

Furth, H. "Young Children's Understanding of Society." In H. McGurk (ed.), *Issues in Childhood Social Development*. London: Methuen, 1978.

Inhelder, B., and Piaget, J. *The Growth of Logical Thinking from Childhood to Adolescence*. New York: Basic Books, 1958.

Kohlberg, L. *Essays on Moral Development*. Vol. 2: *The Psychology of Moral Development*. New York: HarperCollins, 1984.

Laupa, M., and Turiel, E. "Children's Conceptions of Adult and Peer Authority." *Child Development*, 1986, *57*, 405–412.

Ohana, J. "Social Knowledge and Educational Style." Report to the C.N.R.S., Paris, 1987.

Piaget, J. *The Moral Judgment of the Child*. London: Routledge & Kegan Paul, 1932.

Reicher, S., and Emler, N. "Delinquent Behaviour and Attitudes to Formal Authority." *British Journal of Social Psychology*, 1985, *3*, 161–168.

Snarey, J. "The Cross-Cultural Universality of Socio-Moral Development: A Critical Review of Kohlbergian Research." *Psychological Bulletin*, 1985, *97*, 202–232.

Tisak, M. "Children's Conceptions of Parental Authority." *Child Development*, 1986, *57*, 166–176.

Turiel, E. *The Development of Social Knowledge: Morality and Convention*. Cambridge, England: Cambridge University Press, 1983.

Tyler, T. R. *Why People Obey the Law*. New Haven, Conn.: Yale University Press, 1990.

Weber, M. *The Theory of Social and Economic Organizations*. (A. M. Henderson and T. Parsons, trans.) New York: Free Press, 1947.

NICHOLAS EMLER is professor of social psychology at the University of Dundee, Scotland.

Socialization varies for Chicanos growing up in the social and political orders of different U.S. cities.

Ethnic Identity and Political Consciousness in Different Social Orders

Martín Sánchez Jankowski

During the 1960s, political scientists and psychologists became increasingly interested in how people form an understanding of, and an attachment to, the political system in which they live. Five underlying assumptions characterized this work (Easton and Dennis, 1967, 1969; Greenstein, 1965; Hess and Torney, 1967; Jennings and Niemi, 1968, 1974, 1981; Merelman, 1976). First, because political systems need citizen support, citizens must identify positively with the system. Second, political learning begins in childhood and continues at least through adolescence. Third, once certain attitudes toward politics are established, they persist throughout life. Fourth, because the development of attitudes about politics begins in childhood, the agents with the most influence on learning are those people and institutions with whom a child has the most contact: parents, schools, peers, and the media. Further, these influences operate in conjunction with cognitive and emotional development. Fifth, all children, regardless of socioeconomic factors, are influenced in much the same way by these agents.

The social unrest associated with African Americans, Chicanos, and white youth that occurred from the mid-1960s through the early 1970s led socialization researchers to question the blanket validity of the assumptions outlined above (Greenberg, 1970a, 1970b; Garcia, 1973; Abramson, 1972), especially the notion that the attitudes learned in childhood and adolescence persist into adulthood (Searing, Schwartz, and Lind, 1973; Searing, Wright, and Rabinowitz, 1976). The research that followed divided primarily along two lines. One set of studies continued to analyze the family, schools, peers, and the media and certain aspects of individual psychosocial development in order to ascertain whether minority children were socialized differently from white children, and the reasons for their lack of trust in government (Niemi and Associates, 1974; Jennings and Niemi, 1974, 1981; Atkin, 1981). Another set of studies investigated whether the experience of certain political events was especially important in the development of an individual's understanding and disposition toward politics (Sears and McConahay, 1973; Sigel, 1965; Sigel and Brookes, 1974).

The problem was that these studies failed to take the sociopolitical context into consideration. The first set of studies failed to see that the influence of family, schools, peers, the media, and psychosocial development occurs within a particular set of socioeconomic and political conditions. And the second set of studies failed to appreciate that those large historical events that influence individuals' political learning are experienced within particular sociopolitical contexts. In addition, studies that attempted to determine whether minority children were socialized differently from white children failed to appreciate fully that while the socializing agents were the same for each group, the contexts in which they operated were sufficiently different to produce substantial and meaningful variations in behavior.

In this chapter, I focus on the impact of macro socioeconomic and political conditions on the political learning of a group of individuals from an ethnic-racial minority. In particular, I examine the role of parents, schools and teachers, the media, law enforcement, and large historical events as intermediary agents. Because minority group members learn in the context of a group awareness (as they also acquire that awareness), examination of the particular political learning process of minority groups can help identify the influence of social orders. In particular, this is a study of the different social orders that exist in different cities: San Antonio, Texas; Albuquerque, New Mexico; and Los Angeles.

Some studies have recognized the importance of macro social conditions in influencing the political attitudes and behavior of individuals in society (Marvick, 1965; Katznelson, 1982; Gustafsson, 1974). These researchers contend that the patterning of class and race at the national level has a substantial influence on the behaviors of individuals at the local urban level. In their view, political learning is a function of the ascriptive place that an individual's group has in the national context. In this scenario, while we would expect some idiosyncrasies among individuals of a particular ethnicity, race, or social class to occur at the local level, the general pattern of learning would be relatively the same. For example, the majority of U.S. African Americans would be politically socialized in a relatively similar fashion, as would people of lower-class background. I have argued elsewhere that this approach overlooks or underestimates the impact of the local community—the environment with which individuals have the most contact and the one that most influences their day-to-day lives (Jankowski, 1986). Furthermore, because local urban environments vary considerably in socioeconomic and political conditions, it is the local community and its macro socioeconomic variations that must be the focus of attention in order to understand how individuals (especially ethnic-racial group members) are politically socialized. My argument here is that, politically, ethnic-racial group members are socialized first and foremost by their perceptions of and interaction in the social orders that exist in the cities where they reside. Agents such as parents, schools and teachers, peers, and the media (through their reflection of this social order) act as intermediaries in the socializing process.

The chapter uses data gathered as part of a longitudinal study of the political socialization of Chicanos in the Southwest United States (Jankowski, 1986). Three panels of respondents were sampled. The first, in 1976, included 1,040 Chicano respondents from San Antonio, Albuquerque, and Los Angeles who were seventeen- and eighteen-year-old high school seniors in that year. The second, in 1982, included a random sample of 300 respondents (100 from each city) drawn from the original 1,040. And the third, in 1986, included the same 300 (all were accounted for) from the prior two panels who were by then twenty-seven and twenty-eight years of age.

There were two instruments of data collection in the 1976 panel: a questionnaire that all respondents completed (the schedule requiring about one hour and thirty minutes) and in-depth interviews (ninety minutes in duration) with 200 individuals who were chosen from the respondents completing the questionnaire. In the 1982 and 1986 panels, 300 individuals were interviewed using a formal questionnaire and an in-depth interview. The data from the questionnaire have been used in other analyses (Jankowski, 1986, 1988, in press); in this chapter, I primarily rely on the data from the in-depth interviews because they provide understanding of the dynamics involved in political learning.

The Social Orders of Local Urban Environments

Almost every city or urban area has a distinctive social and political environment, which includes certain predictable patterns of social and political interaction. Each urban area can thus be thought of as having a particular "social order." The social order of cities subsumes two other macrolevel conditions. First, it includes and complements the structure of economic activity in a particular city, regulating the pattern of economic relations. Second, it subsumes the political culture of the local environment, including the values and mores that define what is acceptable thought and action in the political arena, as well as the appropriate sanctions for those who violate these norms. The social order establishes the educational agendas in which political learning occurs and is critical in the socialization process.

While the social order is important for everyone who lives in the urban area, it is particularly important for those individuals who are members of an ethnic group because it provides the conditions that influence their opportunities.

The social order of a local environment is formed primarily as a result of five factors: (1) the economic organization of the city and the social structure that supports it, (2) the city's ethnic composition, (3) the history of ethnic relations, (4) the degree of openness of the political system, and (5) the codes (legal system) established and the methods by which they are enforced to control the population. While there may exist among cities a number of social order types, three in particular were explored in the present study: caste oriented, class oriented, and mass oriented. These labels were chosen because the social structures of each city investigated exhibited social relations closely associated with (not identical to) caste, class, and mass social systems. In earlier work, I found three patterned and distinct attitudinal responses toward various political concepts and issues among the individuals who lived in the cities, characterized by the three social orders (Jankowski, 1986). What follows in this chapter is a description of the patterned attitudinal responses and a discussion of some of the influences that social orders have on the political learning of Chicanos and perhaps of other ethnic minorities.

Social Orders and Political Learning

The respondents in the study were asked in both the questionnaire and interview sessions a variety of questions concerning their politics, ranging from attitudes toward ideologies to positions involving political parties and different modes of political participation. In this chapter, I concentrate on ideologies. Respondents were asked both what their images or concepts were of each of a number of ideologies and what their affect was toward them. The respondents' attitudes toward the various ideologies discussed in this chapter formed a pattern that was consistent with the pattern of attitudes found (but not discussed here) toward other aspects of politics about which they were asked in the interviews (see Jankowski, 1986, 1988).

When the respondents in all three cities were asked about their attitudes toward various ideologies—capitalism and liberal democracy, Chicano nationalism, and socialism—a very small proportion in each city was positive about socialism. The respondents understood capitalism and liberal democracy as equivalent to the present American political-economic system and Chicano nationalism as the antithesis of that system. More than half of the respondents in each city were positive about capitalism and liberal democracy, and a smaller percentage were positive about Chicano nationalism-separatism. Probably the most important pattern of response concerns the differences between cities because even the class differences within a city have characteristics that are uniquely associated with the specific city of which they are a part. The adolescents from San Antonio were overwhelmingly positive toward capitalism and liberal democracy and negative toward Chicano nationalism, regardless of their social class standing or the time that they had lived in the city. However, in Albuquerque, the middle-class respondents were more positive toward capitalism and liberal democracy and negative toward Chicano nationalism, whereas the lower-class respondents were more positive toward Chicano nationalism and more negative toward capitalism and liberal democracy. This pattern of attitudinal differences between social classes in Albuquerque held regardless of the length of time that the respondents had lived in Albuquerque. Finally, for Los Angeles, there was variation in attitudinal support for both ideologies among respondents of different social class standing, and this variation was affected by the length of time that the respondents had lived in the city. Specifically, those respondents who had lived in Los Angeles for ten years or more were more likely to be positive toward Chicano nationalism and negative toward capitalism and liberal democracy than were those who had lived in the city for less than ten years. These patterns in the data can be attributed to the influence of the social orders of these cities (Jankowski, 1986). Furthermore, analyses of the data from the 1982 and 1986 panels concerning attitude change and stability (Jankowski, 1988, in press) show a continuing pattern associated with the city of residence.

As individuals develop within their city's social order, they learn the parameters of this order, and the cues by which to identify appropriate attitudes and behaviors concerning certain political issues. One of the first things that they learn is their group's place (historical and contemporary) in the social order (Tajfel, 1981), including not only the social status of their group vis-à-vis other groups but also how the economy of the city works. They learn how the labor market relates to their families and to themselves as extensions of the position of their group vis-à-vis other groups in the social order (Tajfel, 1982; Hogg and Abrams, 1988). By the time they get to high school, they have assessed the economic opportunities that are available to them and their chances for improving their lives. They also have thought about what they have to do to secure the type of jobs that they want. Their knowledge of and attitudes toward the political system are directly related to their knowledge of their socioeconomic situation and their prospects for economic security in the future. They learn in school about the formal governmental institutions of their city and the nation, but even before they get to school they learn what the system considers acceptable attitudes and behavior for their social group.

If the macro conditions associated with social orders have such a strong impact on the socialization of these Chicano young people, how is this impact achieved? Here, we turn to the data provided from the in-depth interviews and focus especially on the factors that were salient during the early learning stage.

The Chicanos in this study identified three means by which they first learned about politics: observation, listening, and personal action. Forty-two percent of those interviewed in the 1976 panel said that they began to learn about the socioeconomic and political system by observing how people related to them as individuals and as members of a particular ethnic-racial group. Most of these individuals said that they had compared how people acted toward them, toward other Chicanos, and toward Anglos. These comparative observations served in part to establish the knowledge of their group's place within the existing social order. Take the comments of Dona, the seventeen-year-old daughter of a mason in San Antonio: "I first learned about politics by watching how the different Anglos would treat Chicanos. Before I knew anything about how the American government worked, I could tell Chicanos didn't have much say in how things got done 'cause of the way Anglo people would treat us." Consider also the comments of Tomás, the eighteen-year-old son of a construction worker in Albuquerque: "Well you know I learned about politics by just looking at how Chicanos lived and how Anglos lived—there was a big difference! Then I noticed that there were some Chicanos who had a lot of what the Anglos had and they also had a lot of say in how things worked in Albuquerque. Right then I knew if you're a Chicano and you got money, then you get more respect from the Anglo and they give you more power."

Listening was also an important technique in acquiring information about politics. Forty-seven percent of those interviewed said that they first began learning about politics by listening to what various people were saying about it and relating it to what they saw. However, only 8 percent said that they started to learn about the system as a result of listening alone, reinforcing the finding that both observation and listening worked together to influence how these Chicanos began the process of understanding their political world.

For the third means, personal action, only 10 percent said they had *first* learned about politics through their activities. Three types of activities were mentioned: overt political action such as participating in picket lines, boycotts, and protests; activities with family and friends as they engaged in various political work; and individual personal experience such as being stopped by the police. Each of these experiences provided the individuals with an awareness of how the system reacts to certain types of political causes and activities. The comments of Guadalupe, the eighteen-year-old daughter of a teacher in Los Angeles, are illustrative:

> I tell you, I started to learn about politics listening to what people had to say about various things. I tried to look around to see if it was the way some people were saying and it kind of was. I mean it was difficult to

see exactly, you know what I mean? Then one time, my sister asked me if I wanted to go with her on a protest of the way schools were being run and I said sure. Well, I tell you, it was an eye-opener for me. I learned real good how things worked. All kinds of people were there. There were politicians, police, some business guys, and some people from the community. You could see it all in front of you and the way things happened told me how things work here.

Role of Family, Schools, Peers, and the Media

In this section I briefly discuss how family, school, and media interact with the local social order to influence respondents' attitudes toward ideologies.

Family. In their classic study of the influence of families and schools on the political attitudes of adolescents, Jennings and Niemi (1974) reported that families had little impact. This conclusion may well be misleading because they looked at the *direct* impact of parents on adolescents' attitudes. In the present study, parents were found to have a significant impact, but not as a result of trying to influence their children to support a certain political party or to think in a specific way about politics. Rather, 64 percent of those interviewed said that their parents either encouraged or discouraged certain attitudes or types of involvement. There was a good deal of variation among individuals from different social class backgrounds. Respondents from middle-class backgrounds reported that their parents generally warned them that certain types of attitudes and behaviors could lead to their being labeled trouble makers, and that this could hurt them in their schools and adversely affect their chances of going on to college. In addition, some of these middle-class adolescents said that they were afraid of expressing support for various political groups or ideologies that were considered radical for fear that their actions would be used by those in power to penalize their parents. Raymundo, the seventeen-year-old son of an office worker in Albuquerque, said, "My dad would tell me, when there were stories about Chicano nationalist groups in the paper or TV, not to join or look like I supported them because one of his bosses might recognize me and take it out on him. You know, he would tell me that if me or my brothers got involved, that his bosses or other people in business might limit the opportunities for him to advance. So I tried to avoid being around any nationalist stuff so that it wouldn't hurt him from getting ahead."

Lower-class adolescents in all three cities most often said as well that their parents warned them against becoming involved in radical politics, but for fear that they would be hurt physically. Julian, the seventeen-year-old son of a hospital worker in San Antonio, said, "My mom and dad used to say don't get involved in a lot of the radical politics stuff because the police will beat you bad if they catch you." However, some of the lower-class adolescents in San Antonio said that their parents had voiced concern about losing their own jobs if their bosses were aware that members of their families had participated in radical political activities. Wilma, the eighteen-year-old daughter of a janitor in San Antonio, said, "I really stayed away from La Raza Unida and the nationalists' stuff because my dad and mom said that if I got involved my dad's bosses might fire him." The difference between the lower-class parents' warnings and the warnings espoused by middle-class parents was that lower-class members in San Antonio thought they would be fired, whereas the middle-class members thought their opportunities for advancement and those of their children would be blocked.

It is important to note the impact of the social order here. In San Antonio, where the society is stratified ethnically between Chicanos and Anglos, the economy is dominated by a low-skill service industry, and the political culture is conservative. The Anglo community is wary of any potential threat by Chicanos to secure political and economic power. In this kind of environment, the parents send a message to their children that there are potential physical costs to them (the children) and financial costs to parents if children engage in what is considered unacceptable political behavior. On the other hand, in cities such as Los Angeles, where there is a more diversified and dynamic economy, a society that is ethnically diverse, and a political culture that lacks a dominant position and encourages a great range of attitudes and tolerance, many lower-class parents communicate two rather divergent messages to their children. Although they warn them not to become involved in the kinds of politics that would limit their opportunities in school or the labor market, they also encourage them to do whatever seems best for themselves regardless of whether it is radical or not. In particular, the latter position was taken by parents who had lived in Los Angeles for ten years or more and who were so frustrated by their inability to become socioeconomically mobile that they communicated their frustration to their children. Regina, the seventeen-year-old daughter of a single mother on welfare, stated that "my mother told me to do whatever was best for me. She told me that I didn't owe anybody anything, and that included the government. She said the government didn't do anything to help us improve so there was no reason to do anything to support it either."

Schools. The schools, through their curricula, and the teachers who interpret and execute those curricula also are influenced by the prevailing social order. As members of specific ethnic groups, they are subject to the same pressures to conform as are other members of the society, perhaps even greater pressures because they are entrusted by the general public to educate all children. In most respects, the curricula of each of the social studies classes that I observed were similar in that they all tried to build an appreciation of the American political system and capitalism. However, while each of the curricula was similar in attempting to build allegiance to the political system, the teachers displayed wide variation in the manner in which they executed the curricula. In most cases, the curriculum implemented by the teacher was that of the prevailing political culture. In San Antonio, the teachers concentrated on teaching students to identify with the political system. Aided by a curriculum that included a course on the free enterprise system, they attempted to delegitimize other ideologies such as socialism and communism by stressing that both were antithetical to every aspect of the American way of life. Furthermore, they avoided the topic of Chicano nationalism, even though the movement had received a great deal of support from Chicanos in Texas (Schockley, 1974). The teachers understood that given the prevailing socioeconomic conditions of Chicanos in San Antonio, the political situation was always potentially explosive around ethnic issues (and nationalism was seen as a threat). Given the political culture, their job was simply to build allegiance to the system. Of course, by characterizing other, competing ideologies as antithetical to the American nation-state, the teachers gave the students the impression that supporters of these ideologies are anti-American and susceptible to some type of sanction. Nearly all of the respondents from San Antonio said that was the message that they received from their courses. Some of the students thought that what the teachers said about nationalism, socialism, and communism was correct. Others thought that it was not necessarily the case that support of another ideology is anti-American. However, all agreed that the teachers had presented such support as anti-American.

In the cities of Los Angeles and Albuquerque, the teachers displayed greater variation in implementing the curricula. In Los Angeles, there were teachers who taught strict allegiance to the present political system in the same manner as that of the teachers in San Antonio. There were others who recognized that the American political system has discriminated against Chicanos, and they gave positive presentations to contending ideologies such as Chicano nationalism and socialism. It is noteworthy that these different teaching approaches were observed among different teachers in the same school, indicating that in Los Angeles the political culture accommodates variation in political attitudes and behaviors as long as no one ideology becomes large enough to challenge the rules of the game.

In Albuquerque, teachers displayed a mixture of the pattern found in San Antonio and Los Angeles, with social class composition of the school as the primary factor determining teachers' style of curriculum implementation. Those teachers who taught in lower-class schools with high enrollments of Chicano students were more likely to be liberal in their approach to civic education. Those who taught in middle-class schools that were ethnically mixed tended to take a more conservative approach (similar to that found in San Antonio). This pattern was consistent with the political culture of Albuquerque, which emphasizes and encourages the kind of class-based politics discussed by Lipset (1963) in terms of "democratic class struggle" within the present electoral system. In Albuquerque, the political culture seems to support the notion that those who become middle class, regardless of ethnicity, should support the Republican Party. It is true that not many of the respondents in the 1976 panel identified themselves as Republicans, but the political culture encourages individuals to think about what is best for their social class standing. Given this bias in the political culture, after the 1976 panel interviews I predicted that when the Raza Unida party ceased to exist (which happened after the 1978 Texas gubernatorial election), the political arena would revert back to the Republican and Democratic parties, and middle-class Chicano interests would drift to the Republicans. In elections from 1980 through 1988 that prediction was substantiated.

Peers and the Media. Most of the peer groups in the present study tended to reinforce the prevailing attitudes within the social friendship networks. Even when a group of peers outside one person's friendship network expressed support for political positions that the individual found threatening, this exerted an influence toward greater commitment to existing attitudes. This tendency for both positive and negative reinforcement to strengthen commitment to existing attitudes is unusual. One possible explanation is that, because Chicanos have faced persistent socioeconomic and political discrimination, their political attitudes are more directly linked to their strategies for making a better life for themselves. A negative peer reinforcement leads them to defensively strengthen their commitment to their views. Another explanation, which may be complementary, is that by failing to examine more than one peer group for an individual, previous research has failed to capture the complexity in these influences.

Studies that have attempted to assess the influence of media in the socialization process have generally had difficulty in identifying their roles and in estimating the relative directness of their effects. The findings from the present study strongly suggest that the media play less of a direct role in establishing political attitudes than they do in reinforcing attitudes that already exist. For example, in all three cities, the respondents reported that the television news programs they watched, the radio news programs to which they listened, and the newspapers they read presented information that was congruous with what most of the people in their cities believed.

In sum, it is not parents, teachers, peers, or media who directly teach individuals about politics but rather the local political environment with which they interact. Parents, teachers, peers, and media are themselves influenced by this environment, and ultimately they reinforce the political culture of the prevailing social order of their city by modeling what they see as appropriate behavior and cautioning their adolescent children against what they see as inappropriate behavior.

Impact of Social Order Socialization over Time

Early socialization studies were based on the assumption that what a person learned in the early part of his or her life had great stability over time. More recent thinking concerning early childhood socialization suggests that it has little impact on a person's political attitudes in adulthood because individuals continue the process of political socialization throughout their lives (Cook, 1985). Still, however, the question remains of whether one's early learning in life influences politics in adulthood (see Sears, 1990). One of the primary aims of the present longitudinal study has been to address this question. Although only three panels of the study have been completed, covering ten years of the respondents' lives (from seventeen and eighteen years of age to twenty-seven and twenty-eight years of age), these data suggest a great deal of stability in the political attitudes of the individuals over the ten-year period and thus support the theoretical position that the effects of early socialization last into adulthood. However, at the same time, there are some individuals in the sample who have experienced significant changes in their attitudes (Jankowski, in press).

These attitudinal changes were stimulated by two factors. First, changes in respondents' socioeconomic standing (particularly, upward mobility) motivated them to stop supporting various positions associated with radical politics and to begin supporting the existing political system. Second, changes in what were considered the major issues in the community affected people's political attitudes. For example, there was a tendency to stop supporting certain positions associated with nationalist politics because they no longer were considered salient within the community, corroborating a finding by Latouche (1985) among Quebec radicals. However, the changes that occurred among the respondents of the present study were mostly within the limits established by the political cultures and social orders of the respective environments. There were very few changes that occurred outside of what was considered applicable by the local political culture. This limitation suggests that individuals are socialized originally by their local social orders and learn the local political geography in order to navigate effectively through it. At the same time, they integrate national symbols into the local political culture because the local environment is the arena in which most individuals find these symbols played out. Thus, we are likely to observe a great deal of stability in attitudes of individuals over time because the social orders (and the concomitant political cultures) of most young people do not change very much over time. However, we are also likely to witness some changes as individuals develop through their lives, especially if they move to different social orders. These changes can be minor or they can be quite radical, but all of them relate to two aspects of earlier socialization: (1) the extent to which the individual is socialized and (2) the environment of that early socialization as compared to the environments experienced during later periods.

Concerning the first point, the present data suggest that there are two tiers in the socialization process. That is, every political system attempts to socialize its citizens to support it through two processes. First, there is the attempt to teach every individual to identify acceptable and unacceptable political attitudes and behaviors. Here, the various social and political agents of the society (parents, teachers, officials, media, and so on) provide examples of acceptable political attitudes and examples of threatening and therefore unacceptable attitudes. Although the examples presented by these agents may be critical of the political system, these examples can be used by the system to justify itself, such as by demonstrating its tolerance. In addition, the social agents provide examples of and a rationale for the punishments that the state administers for unacceptable attitudes and behavior. In this manner, the political parameters governing citizen attitudes and behavior are clarified.

Second, governments attempt to foster in each individual the values underlying the political system. These values are the ethical elements that clarify the way a political system "should" be, or the way a political system "ought" to operate. For example, in the United States, communism has been portrayed as morally and politically flawed because of its opposition to private property and religion; and those who support and proselytize it have been presented as demons (Rogin, 1987).

Systems can achieve the desired objective of compliance when either one of these two processes of socialization is implemented. In the present study, 58 percent of the individuals interviewed had been socialized to the system through the first tier of the process, as evidenced by their comments that they were aware that any challenges by them to the system might bring negative sanctions on them and/or their families. The state and system receives compliance from these individuals, but not necessarily loyalty (Sniderman, 1981). Thus, what appear to be sudden shifts in attitudes among these individuals between support for conventional and for radical forms of politics are attributable to their first-tier political learning ("the rules of the game") during socialization. These individuals comply with the political system, but primarily out of fear of the punishments assessed by the state for violations of the rules. It is thus these same individuals who at other times may be influenced by political movements that challenge the authority or legitimacy of the dominant political system, especially when certain socioeconomic and political conditions are present, such as the state's inability to effectively administer punishments.

The second tier of socialization is by far the most powerful in the maintenance of political systems because it encourages compliance through the internal controls exercised by the individual rather than by the external agency of the state. Therefore, the state can rely on loyalty (Sniderman, 1981) when individuals have incorporated the values underlying the political system and made them into personal values.

Changes in attitudes over the life course can occur when individuals leave one type of social order and move to another, or when their social orders are in the process of change. For these individuals, attitudinal stability is likely associated with their past places of residence, and attitudes then change to bring them into accord with the social orders in which they now live. Other things being equal, the magnitude of attitudinal shift depends on the degree of difference that exists between the earlier and the later social orders. When the individual moves to another locale, the process of initial socialization is often reenacted: identifying the political geography and one's attitudinal position within that geography and readjusting any attitudes understood as inappropriate for the present environment so that they more closely coincide with appropriate attitudes. Early socialization may not succeed in maintaining specific attitudes over the life course, but it is able to maintain the same process of defining what attitudes are appropriate in a particular social order.

The data in the present study concern Chicanos, but the processes of interaction in the local social order discussed here apply to other ethnic or racial minority groups in the United States. It is quite likely that they apply to ethnic and racial groups in other multi-ethnic countries as well. In order to assess the generalizability of the present findings, similarly designed longitudinal studies must be conducted in different areas and among other ethnic groups. In this way, we can acquire a better understanding of whether the conceptual framework applies to the social orders of groups delineated by national or religious affiliation, such as Italians, Irish, and Jews.

References

Abramson, P. "Political Efficacy and Political Trust Among Black School Children: Two Explanations." *Journal of Politics,* 1972, *34,* 1243–1275.

Atkin, C. "Communication and Political Socialization." In D. Nimmo and K. Sanders (eds.), *Handbook of Political Communication.* Newbury Park, Calif.: Sage, 1981.

Cook, T. E. "The Bear Market in Political Socialization and the Costs of Misunderstood Psychological Theories." *American Political Science Review,* 1985, *79,* 1079–1093.

Easton, D., and Dennis, J. "The Child's Acquisition of Regime Norms: Political Efficacy." *American Political Science Review,* 1967, *61,* 25–38.

Easton, D., and Dennis, J. *Children in the Political System: Origins of Political Legitimacy.* New York: McGraw-Hill, 1969.

Garcia, F. C. *The Political Socialization of Chicano Children.* New York: Praeger, 1973.

Greenberg, E. "Black Children and the Political System." *Public Opinion Quarterly,* 1970a, *34,* 333–345.

Greenberg, E. "Children and the Political Community: A Comparison Across Racial Lines." *Midwest Journal of Political Science,* 1970b, *14,* 249–275.

Greenstein, F. I. *Children and Politics.* New Haven, Conn.: Yale University Press, 1965.

Gustafsson, G. "Environmental Influence on Political Learning." In R. Niemi and Associates (eds.), *The Politics of Future Citizens: New Dimensions in the Political Socialization of Children.* San Francisco: Jossey-Bass, 1974.

Hess, R. D., and Torney, J. V. *The Development of Political Attitudes in Children.* Hawthorne, N.Y.: Aldine, 1967.

Hogg, M. P., and Abrams, D. *Social Identifications: A Social Psychology of Intergroup Relations and Group Processes.* New York: Routledge, 1988.

Jankowski, M. S. *City Bound: Urban Life and Political Attitudes Among Chicano Youth.* Albuquerque: University of New Mexico Press, 1986.

Jankowski, M. S. "Change and Stability in Political Attitudes Among Chicanos: A Panel Study, 1976-1986." Paper presented at the annual meeting of the Western Political Science Association, San Francisco, April 1988.

Jankowski, M. S. "Where Have All the Nationalists Gone?" In D. Montejano (ed.), *Chicano Politics and Society.* Albuquerque: University of New Mexico Press, in press.

Jennings, M. K., and Niemi, R. G. "The Transformation of Political Values from Parent to Child." *American Political Science Review,* 1968, *62,* 169-184.

Jennings, M. K., and Niemi, R. G. *The Political Character of Adolescence.* Princeton, N.J.: Princeton University Press, 1974.

Jennings, M. K., and Niemi, R. G. *Generations and Politics.* Princeton, N.J.: Princeton University Press, 1981.

Katznelson, I. *City Trenches: Urban Politics and the Patterning of Class in the United States.* Chicago: University of Chicago Press, 1982.

Latouche, D. "Jeunesse et nationalisme au Quebec: Une Ideologie peut-ille mourir" [Youth and nationalism in Quebec: Can an ideology be permitted to die?]. *Revue Francaise de Science Politique,* 1985, *35,* 236-260.

Lipset, S. M. *Political Man: The Social Bases of Politics.* Garden City, N.Y.: Anchor Books, 1963.

Marvick, D. "The Political Socialization of the Negro American." *Annals of the American Academy of Political and Social Sciences,* 1965, *361,* 112-127.

Merelman, R. *Political Reasoning in Adolescence: Some Bridging Themes.* Newbury Park, Calif.: Sage, 1976.

Niemi, R. G., and Associates. (eds.). *The Politics of Future Citizens: New Dimensions in the Political Socialization of Children.* San Francisco: Jossey-Bass, 1974.

Rogin, M. P. *Ronald Reagan the Movie: And Other Episodes in Political Demonology.* Berkeley and Los Angeles: University of California Press, 1987.

Schockley, J. *Chicano Revolt in a Texas Town.* South Bend, Ind.: University of Notre Dame Press, 1974.

Searing, D. D., Schwartz, J. J., and Lind, A. E. "The Structuring Principle: Political Socialization and Belief Systems." *American Political Science Review,* 1973, *67,* 415-432.

Searing, D. D., Wright, G., and Rabinowitz, G. "The Primacy Principle: Attitude Change and Political Socialization." *British Journal of Political Science,* 1976, *6,* 83-113.

Sears, D. O. "Whither Political Socialization Research?" In O. Ichilov (ed.), *Political Socialization, Citizenship Education, and Democracy.* New York: Teachers College Press, 1990.

Sears, D. O., and McConahay, J. B. *The Politics of Violence: The New Urban Blacks and the Watts Riot.* Boston: Houghton Mifflin, 1973.

Sigel, R. "An Exploration into Some Aspects of Political Socialization: School Children's Reactions to the Death of a President." In M. Wolfenstein and G. Kliman (eds.), *Children and the Death of a President.* New York: Doubleday, 1965.

Sigel, R., and Brookes, M. "Becoming Critical About Politics." In R. Niemi and Associates (eds.), *The Politics of Future Citizens: New Dimensions in the Political Socialization of Children.* San Francisco: Jossey-Bass, 1974.

Sniderman, P. M. *A Question of Loyalty.* Berkeley and Los Angeles: University of California Press, 1981.

Tajfel, H. *Human Groups and Social Categories.* Cambridge, England: Cambridge University Press, 1981.

Tajfel, H. (ed.). *Social Identity and Intergroup Relations.* Cambridge, England: Cambridge University Press, 1982.

MARTÍN SÁNCHEZ JANKOWSKI is associate professor of sociology at the University of California, Berkeley.

Socialization is influenced by the social and political ecology of young adults in the United States.

Young Adults' Understanding of Political Issues: A Social-Ecological Analysis

Judith Van Hoorn, Paula J. LeVeck

What is the relation between young adults' constructions of knowledge about the changing international political situation and their social environments? In this chapter, we describe the interplay between the dynamic, developing nature of three young adults and the dynamic, changing nature of the social systems of which they are a part, using concepts from the social-ecological perspective proposed by Bronfenbrenner (1979).

The three case studies here cover late adolescence in a university setting through early adulthood and entrance into the worlds of work and parenthood. Findings are based on data collected from 1983 through early 1990 as part of a larger, ongoing longitudinal survey-interview study. The three individuals discussed here, like most respondents in this study, changed in their patterns of response to attitude survey items about world issues, paralleling changes in patterns in national U.S. polls during the same period. However, the particular reasons given by different individuals as they expressed their opinions reflected each individual's unique social ecology.

Social-Ecological Perspective

Why do Americans react to political events in the ways that they do? How do their knowledge, feelings, and behavioral responses relate to the diverse contexts of their lives? Although the biographies of famous political figures in part provide detailed answers to these questions, the portraits drawn are exceptional cases, revealing little about how the political perspective of ordinary people is influenced by their social contexts. Bronfenbrenner's

(1979) social-ecological model, with its multidimensional analysis of social contexts, enables researchers to differentiate among various environmental levels and to assess their impact on the individual and the impact of the individual on them.

Bronfenbrenner's (1979, p. 3) definition of human development emphasizes the relationship between the individual and the social context: "Development is . . . a lasting change in the way in which a person perceives and deals with his environment. . . . The ecological environment [in which development takes place] is conceived of as a set of nested structures, each inside the next, like a set of Russian dolls." At the center of this nested structure are the microsystems in which the person is directly involved in particular roles, activities, and face-to-face interactions. Microsystems are the "pattern of activities, roles and interpersonal relations experienced by the developing person in a given setting with particular physical and material characteristics" (p. 22). Examples of microsystems include the home, classroom, and office. As people mature, they participate in a greater number of microsystems. As individuals develop, they experience changes in roles and activities within microsystems, for example, the change from living with one's family to living in one's own apartment. Changes of this kind are termed *ecological transitions* (p. 26).

The next level is the mesosystem. "The mesosystem comprises the interrelationship between two or more settings [microsystems] in which the developing person actively participates . . . [for example] for an adult, among family, work and social life" (p. 25). The mesosystem concept is important since it allows one to describe both consistencies and differences among microsystems.

The third level, the exosystem, consists of the "settings that do not involve the developing person as an active participant but in which events occur that affect, or are affected by, what happens [in the individual's microsystem]" (p. 237). Bronfenbrenner emphasizes establishing a causal relationship, for example, that a particular event in the macrosystem effects a change in the microsystem, which in turn affects an individual's development.

The most encompassing system is the macrosystem: "The consistency observed within a given culture or subculture in the form and content of its constituent micro-, meso-, and exosystems, as well as any belief systems or ideology underlying such consistencies" (p. 258). For example, across the United States, one would expect to find similarities in expectations for employees in a given profession or in ideologies relating to the role of women in politics.

The Study

A total of 1,239 respondents originally participated in our 1983 survey on awareness of and reaction to the threat of nuclear war (Van Hoorn and

French, 1986). To better understand the factors that influence college students' political socialization, we selected and recontacted, in 1986–1987, a small sample ($N = 41$) of students who had participated in the original survey and who represented a broad range of viewpoints. All were students at two universities, one public and one private. In addition to a questionnaire, we conducted one- to two-hour personal interviews in which participants reflected on their answers to the survey items and gave their own explanations for the similarities and differences between their 1983 responses and their 1986–1987 responses (Van Hoorn, LeVeck, and French, 1989).

In early 1990, we carried out a third investigation of this group (and the second set of interviews). Twenty-three of the forty-one participants interviewed in 1986–1987 were located, and all participated. Eleven participants, all of whom lived within one hundred miles of the campuses, were interviewed in person; the other twelve took part in shorter, telephone interviews.

Global Events and U.S. Perceptions

During the interviews in the present study, participants were asked to discuss sociopolitical changes. We present the following brief summary of global events in the 1980s and U.S. perceptions of them as a context for the respondents' comments.

In the early 1980s, the Reagan administration's perception of the USSR is illustrated by President Reagan's depiction of Soviet leaders as liars and cheaters and the Soviet Union as an "evil empire" (Bell, 1989). However, by 1987, the Intermediate-Range Nuclear Forces Treaty was signed and, in 1988, Reagan said, "I think that through this succession of summits there is a better understanding" ("Images, Pictures of 1988," 1988, p. 64). In 1989–1990, as communist regimes toppled in Eastern Europe and steps toward democratization were taken by several countries, and as arms reductions negotiations continued, the "end of the Cold War" was a popular phrase in the United States. The period from 1983 to 1990 was also marked by other significant global events: the U.S. invasion of Grenada, armed conflicts in El Salvador and Nicaragua, the Soviet downing of Korean Airlines Flight 007, the Iran-Contra affair, the U.S. bombing of Libya, and the Chernobyl nuclear disaster.

As recently as 1988, when Americans were asked to name the greatest threat to U.S. national security, most named military or foreign policy issues. But, by early 1990, when asked to name the top two threats to the United States, nonmilitary issues such as drug traffic, pollution, crime, health care costs, and federal budget deficits were chosen 90 percent of the time, and military issues such as Third World nuclear weapons and the Mideast and Central American conflicts were selected only 51 percent of the time (Kiley and Marttila, 1990).

Study Findings

In each of the twenty-three interviews conducted in early 1990, the participants' constructions of knowledge about four global topics were elicited: (1) major world changes between 1986–1987 and early 1990, (2) major problems facing the world in early 1990, (3) feelings about the USSR, and (4) the likelihood of a nuclear war between the United States and the USSR in the next fifty years. The most frequently mentioned major world changes since the 1986–1987 interviews concerned political events in other countries, notably the political restructuring of Eastern Europe. Second, respondents mentioned improved relations between the United States and the USSR, and, third, the removal of the Berlin Wall.

When asked to name the greatest current worldwide problems, participants identified (in rank order) the environment (global warming, pollution, destruction of rain forests, toxic wastes, and so on), world hunger, drugs, poverty and economic instability, religious wars and fanaticism, and population growth. The nuclear arms race was named less frequently than any of the problems above. These problems parallel those identified in a national U.S. poll, from military and foreign policy subjects in the mid-1980s to global environmental and quality-of-life concerns by the late 1980s, although the rank ordering of topics is not identical (Kiley and Marttilla, 1990). Respondents in our study perceived a decrease in the threat of a nuclear confrontation with the USSR and shifted toward more positive feelings about the Soviet Union, again parallel to findings in the U.S. poll.

The following case studies describe individuals' views and perceptions from 1986–1987 to 1990, as examined from Bronfenbrenner's social-ecological perspective. These profiles were chosen because they illustrate different microsystems and macrosystems, including ideologies regarding world events.

Susan: The Future Generation. At the time of the interview in 1990, Susan was twenty-five years old and a single mother of a two-year-old son. She was working toward an undergraduate degree in economics and was a part-time employee at the state university. She described herself as a "hard-working, independent, sensitive, tough, thoughtful, and reasonably intelligent individual."

Interview Responses in January 1990. In response to the question "What do you see as the major changes that have occurred in the world since our last interview [in 1986–1987]?" Susan answered, in part, "All of the things that have been happening in Eastern Europe . . . the Chinese students [Tiananmen Square demonstrations] . . . I think the whole world is seeing that democracy is a better way to go. It's created quite a stir." To the question "What do you see as the greatest problems facing the world?"— asked only in 1990—she responded, "I think hunger is a major problem . . . enormous problem. . . . Women's inequality, minority inequality . . . any injustice that happens. I think the environment is a huge problem . . .

the burning of rain forests, toxic waste, pollution, landfills . . . dirty needles washing up on the beach." When asked, in 1986–1987, "All in all, how do you feel about the USSR?" she answered, "Dislike it somewhat. . . . I don't really think that I would want to live under that kind of system." But by 1990, she had changed her opinion: "Like it somewhat. . . . I don't think they are any different than we are. . . . I think they have made some mistakes in the past that they are trying to make up for now and so I wouldn't say that I love it, but I think they are working [toward democratization]." Finally, when asked, in 1983 and again in 1986–1987, "In the next fifty years, how likely do you think it is that the United States will be involved in a nuclear war with the Soviet Union?" she answered, "Somewhat likely." But, by 1990, she gave a different response: "Very unlikely. . . . I think that the Cold War is coming closer to an end."

Social-Ecological Analysis. How did Susan's responses regarding these international issues relate to her personal social ecology? Several microsystems seemed influential in the way that she interpreted world events.

Susan lived with her son in an apartment in a small city. She identified his birth as the most significant event in her life between 1987 and 1990: "[It] broadened my social awareness . . . has made a lot of issues more important to me than they were in the past." Her role orientation as a caring, responsible parent greatly determined those aspects of external reality that she regarded as salient and the way in which she constructed their meaning. Susan's selection of hunger, inequality, and the environment as important global issues related to her primary immediate concern, the well-being of her son.

Susan's family of origin was a second microsystem of continuing importance in her life. Although she lived separately, she still resided within a few miles of them and was in frequent contact. She identified the issues of hunger and inequality in relation to the value of "fairness" as stressed by her parents.

The state university that Susan attended is located within a rural, religiously and politically conservative area, with a college culture quiescent around political issues. Susan had, however, been active in the campus Hunger Network, which provided food to poor families in the community.

Her student role was related to another level of community involvement. The professor of her California politics class had arranged for her to intern at the local state senator's office. The professor became the link between the microsystem of the classroom and the microsystem of the senator's office, thus forming a mesosystem. Through this office, Susan was involved in a child health care project that focused on equal access to health services. Her activities at the microsystem of the state senator's office, which directly linked to the more encompassing systems of state government, also illustrated the connection of her desire to help others with her desire to ensure the welfare of her young son. Moreover, these activities related to the inequality that she identified as one of the major problems in the exosystem and macrosystem. It also linked her role as mother in the family system to broader social systems.

Susan's emphasis on democracy as "a better way to go" was the major theme in her responses regarding major world changes. Susan had identified "freedom" as an important value that derived from her family of origin. Her belief in the participatory democratic process was underscored by her volunteer activity at her senator's office.

Susan obtained much of her information about the world from television, newspapers, and a national magazine. These sources may be thought of as expressions of macrosystem political ideologies. For example, in 1983, she thought about the threat of nuclear war "each week." By 1987, this frequency had decreased to "each month" and, by 1990, to "rarely." Susan's construction of knowledge about global issues paralleled the low level of analysis in the popular press and on television. Her opinions were expressed as generalized impressions. She did not attempt to deal with issues comprehensively or systematically, nor did she offer hypotheses for why changes had occurred in the world.

Sarah: The American Dream. Sarah, age twenty-five in 1990, graduated from the private university in 1986, majoring in political science. She was living with her significant other in a major urban area. She worked as a legal assistant in a large corporate law firm and considered her work to be the most important change in her life since graduation.

In 1990, Sarah identified her major personal characteristic as "extremely independent." Her goals were marriage, children, and a small business that would give her flexibility to combine the roles of mother and career woman. Her greatest hopes were to "have an enormous amount of money, and a house, a great big one, have a family, a great big yard, a dog, and a happy settled life."

Interview Responses in January 1990. In response to the question about major changes in the world, Sarah answered, "I think the freedom that happened in the Eastern Bloc and in East Asia as well." In response to the question about the greatest problems facing the world, she said, "Definitely any crippling diseases, from multiple sclerosis to AIDS . . . and homelessness is a definite problem. . . . Not to jump on the homeless bandwagon, but I get pretty sick to my stomach when I walk up any street and I see a mother and child that are homeless asking for money." When asked, in 1986–1987, to describe her feelings about the USSR, she said, "Like it somewhat. . . . I wouldn't want to live there. . . . I guess the people there are nice like any place." In 1990, she said, "I guess I like it somewhat. . . . I feel they are the same, basically, as any other nation, just a little more powerful. Just like the U.S." Finally, in response to the question about the likelihood of nuclear war between the United States and the USSR, she responded "Somewhat likely" in 1983, and "Unlikely" in 1986–1987. In 1990, she said, "Very unlikely. . . . That is because so much has happened . . . change of events."

Social-Ecological Analysis. Sarah identified her family of origin as a source of great influence on her current outlook. She described her parents as working professionals, upper-middle class, and politically conservative.

At the time of the 1986–1987 interview, Sarah attended a private university at which most of the students were also upper-middle class and politically conservative. Her more liberal professors influenced her views during her first two years: "I think when I was a sophomore I was more impressionable. I thought professors were almost like God." She later disagreed with them and prided herself on her independent views. Her later views, however, reflected the prevailing political opinions of her primary microsystem of family and peers.

By 1990, Sarah had made the transition to relationships within other microsystems embedded in the exosystems of the city, but she still expressed values congruent with those of her family and school friends. She was embarked on a career and was developing the intimate relationship that she hoped would lead to marriage and "a happy settled life."

Sarah did not participate in any microsystem involving social or community organizations. She did show a nascent involvement in efforts to ameliorate problems in the urban exosystem in which she resided, donating blood every two months and giving "lots of clothes to the Salvation Army and Goodwill . . . to a lot of people off the street."

Sarah obtained her information about international developments (events within the macrosystem) primarily through television news: "[Television] is the main focal point right now." Her statement "because everybody basically watches TV when they get home" suggested that she chose television as her primary source because it was the choice of her microsystem reference group: sophisticated young adults.

Sarah explained her lack of interest in political actions in 1990: "I can't chain myself to the White House and stuff. . . . I'm not going to attach myself to a warhead or anything." She believed that communication with elected officials was useless because "I don't think you can influence the advisers, and the advisers influence the elected officials, so I really don't think there is any way I could affect it." Sarah indicated little interest in international events, including nuclear issues. Focused on the development of an intimate relationship and a career within her two most important microsystems, she indicated that the more abstract realities were almost irrelevant. Therefore, she did not engage the same cognitive processes that she engaged in analyzing her personal and professional life. For example, she discussed her habit of talking through and reflecting on aspects of her more personal problems: "Debating, like arguing in my mind . . . the steps

I should take . . . then come up with an answer for myself." In contrast, she considered global and national problems, such as the nuclear threat, "more in someone else's hands."

Sarah's lack of involvement in political activity also appeared consistent with the apparent lack of interest displayed by those in her primary microsystems. Her belief that elected officials would not listen to her concerns suggests a lack of feeling connected with a major exosystem.

Sarah's feelings about the USSR also indicated the influence of her family of origin. Her parents had made two trips to the Soviet Union between 1985 and 1990 and had discussed her impressions with her. Indeed, she was one of the few politically conservative students to say that she "liked it" (the USSR) in 1986 as well as in 1990. Sarah viewed herself as more conscious of what was going on in the world in 1990 than she was as a student. This growing awareness may have reflected her ecological transition from the sheltered world of home and university to her life as a working adult in a big city.

"Freedom," the one world change that she mentioned, may have reflected her feeling of growing independence, as well as the headlines in the media. The two world problems that she identified, "crippling diseases" and "homelessness," expressed the same concerns that she had shown in her limited involvement in her own community, through giving blood, donating food, and giving to homeless people on the street. She was outraged at the plight of homeless mothers and children: "I get pretty sick to my stomach. . . . I'm sure it's very humiliating for them. . . . No one wants to be out there like that." This outrage suggests her capacity to respond to problems personally salient to her: homelessness as a glaring manifestation of failure to achieve the American Dream.

Matt: The Family Circle. Matt was a twenty-six-year-old graduate of the private university, who majored in business and public administration. He was single, lived in a large city, and worked for a U.S. government agency investigating charges of discrimination in employment. In 1990, Matt described himself as a person who cared for and wanted to do something for others (for example, the homeless and migrant farm workers). He viewed his identification as Hispanic and Catholic as strong influences on his commitment to care for others.

Interview Responses in January 1990. In response to the question about major changes in the world, Matt answered, "Politically . . . in South Africa . . . some of the people who were jailed, being released. The possibility of Mandela himself being released. . . . The peace that exists and the relations that exist between us and Europe, and us and the Soviet Union. I feel real good about it. That's why I don't fear it [nuclear war] like I did then [1983–1986]." In response to the question about the greatest problems facing the world, he said, "The economic problems. I think it is going to be more difficult for us . . . to achieve economic success. . . . There are other countries that globally can get together and start developing peace with each other . . . relations with other countries. . . . There's a lot to learn about Cuba . . . and I don't think we should always think of them as our enemy. . . . World hunger is a big problem. . . . Civil war in a lot of countries really bothers me, especially the Latin American countries . . . Middle East religious wars. . . . It is sad to see what people have gone through, and with their own people." When asked, in 1986–1987, to describe his feelings about the USSR, he said, "Like it somewhat." In 1990, he said, "I like it somewhat, I don't think I know enough about the USSR to love it." Finally, in response to the question about the likelihood of nuclear war between the United States and the USSR, he responded "Somewhat likely" in 1983. In 1986, he said, "Somewhat likely. . . . If there was to be a nuclear war, the two prime countries . . . would be the U.S. and USSR." But, in 1990, he said, "Unlikely . . . again, going back to the way things are going now."

Social-Ecological Analysis. The impact of Matt's social ecology on his construction of political knowledge was particularly striking in his discussions of the problems of racism and of economic issues such as homelessness. These two themes expressed his family's economic situation and his experiences in the microsystems of his hometown Hispanic community, the university, and his workplace.

In 1990, Matt lived alone in a major urban area but had remained in close contact with his family, who lived nearby. Just prior to the interview, Matt learned that his family's financial situation had seriously worsened: "My family could have been homeless." He had decided that he would buy his family a house in a better part of town, move back home, and help care for his parents and younger siblings.

Matt actively participated in several related microsystems within the exosystem of his hometown Hispanic community that involved contributing to the well-being of others. He also became increasingly active in the Hispanic political community and was asked to run for office.

Matt's transition from the microsystems of the university to the microsystems of the workplace has been very important to him. He identified his job as the most significant change in his life since graduation. His work involved investigations into cases of alleged discrimination in work settings. Matt emphasized that he fit in with the staff at work more than he had fit into the university environment. In college he viewed himself as a poor, Hispanic student with liberal political views and a social conscience. He felt distant from what he perceived as the upper-middle-class, Caucasian, subtly racist, and politically conservative student culture of the university. He was now in a work environment with others who had common views, interests, and values.

During the interview, when naming major world problems and changes, Matt twice mentioned South Africa, a symbol of institutionalized racism. Similarly, in talking about major problems (and also the media), he focused on Latin America. He was the only participant interviewed who discussed minority issues when talking about U.S.-USSR relations: "They are having problems with their own minorities . . . and racial problems. They're not so different from us and I think that needs to be emphasized." He also related his feelings about the USSR to reports brought back from there by a group of Hispanic adolescents from his hometown: "They came back with a real good feeling for the Soviet Union and the people there." Images of other nations in Matt's case, as well as in Sarah's, are mediated by the second-hand experiences of members of a microsystem.

When Matt discussed issues at the level of the macrosystem, he made frequent references to the media as his main source of information. He specifically mentioned the television news program "Nightline," the local news, the local paper, the *Los Angeles Times,* and a Hispanic magazine. Throughout the interview in 1990, Matt spontaneously discussed his view that the media were educational sources that were failing to do their job. The media were seen to influence people by shaping not only what issues were important but also the way in which people thought about them. For example, "I think [that] with regard to the civil wars in Central America and in the Middle East, they're saying, 'This is what's going on. This happened today.' Boom. That's it. I don't think they are doing a good job as educators of why it's going on, why it started. A lot of people don't know why there are Contras and why there are Sandinistas and which one does the U.S. back."

Matt's understanding of how he can personally effect changes at the levels of the macrosystem and the exosystem had changed since graduation. In 1986, he reflected, "I'm not too educated . . . on how an individual can effect certain things nationally," although he acknowledged that he did know how to have an impact at the local level. By 1990, his experience and position at work in particular had helped him develop a greater feeling of efficacy: "I had an interest in learning a little bit more . . . because now it seems to be that I have an opportunity to do something [that will influence local, state, and national policies]."

Conclusion

The past decade has been marked by major changes in the U.S. public's perceptions of important world issues, including U.S.-USSR relations. The changes that we found in the responses of a small and select sample of recent graduates of two California universities paralleled the changes in polls of representative samples of U.S. adults. We wanted to understand factors having an impact on individuals' interpretations of global events, and we used Bronfenbrenner's (1979) model to analyze interview data and to describe how young adults' constructions of political knowledge of international issues related to the multiple systems within their social ecologies.

This perspective has not been widely used to describe adult development nor political socialization.

Participants' interest in and interpretations of the international political issues studied were greatly influenced by their most salient microsystems. When asked to discuss the important world changes that had occurred since their last interview, participants focused on issues in the macrosystem that related to aspects of the microsystem with high cognitive and affective import. The case studies present numerous illustrations. For example, both Matt and Sarah explained their positive views of the Soviet Union by referring to positive reports of visits to the USSR that people from their microsystems had shared with them.

The three case studies demonstrate the fundamental way in which microsystems orient individuals to particular issues in the macrosystem. Matt's concern about poverty and racism at the global level reflected his concern about his own family, poor and Hispanic. When working at her state senator's office, Susan participated in projects that reflected her personal responsibility to care for her son. Sarah's low level of interest in community and national issues reflected the lack of political concern shown by members of her salient microsystems.

The case studies of Matt and Susan also illustrate how individuals affect their environments, not only at the level of the microsystem but at the level of the macrosystem as well, albeit in increments. For example, the outcome of an employment discrimination case that Matt worked on in California might affect a future case in Florida.

As we have shown, the nested systems that Bronfenbrenner describes help to explain the relationship between individuals' personal lives and their understanding of global issues. This perspective could be further differentiated to examine the effects of different levels of the macrosystem (national to global) on microsystems and on individuals' development. Application of the social-ecological perspective to the analysis of adult political socialization would also be useful in mapping the concomitant effects that individuals have on the different systems, from microsystem to macrosystem, in their respective social ecologies.

References

Bell, C. The Reagan Paradox: American Foreign Policy in the 1980s. New Brunswick, N.J.: Rutgers University Press, 1989.

Bronfenbrenner, U. The Ecology of Human Development: Experiments by Nature and Design. Cambridge, Mass.: Harvard University Press, 1979.

"Images, Pictures of 1988." Time Magazine, Dec. 26, 1988, p. 64.

Kiley, T., and Marttila, J. "The Peace Dividend as the Public Sees It." Report No. 1. Winchester, Mass.: Americans Talk Security Project, 1990.

Van Hoorn, J., and French, P. "Facing the Nuclear Threat: Comparisons of Adolescents and Adults." In B. Berger Gould, S. Moon, and J. Van Hoorn (eds.), Growing Up Scared? Berkeley, Calif.: Open Books, 1986.

Van Hoorn, J., LeVeck, P., and French, P. "Transitions in the Nuclear Age." *Journal of Adolescence,* 1989, *12,* 41–53.

JUDITH VAN HOORN *is associate professor, School of Education, University of the Pacific.*

PAULA J. LEVECK *is professor of nursing, California State University, Stanislaus.*

INDEX

Abelson, R. P., 55, 63
Abrams, D., 83, 92
Abramson, P., 79, 91
Adams, G. R., 40, 50
Adelson, J., 4, 10, 29, 38, 40, 44, 50, 54, 62, 68, 77
Adolescents: ethnicity and political consciousness of, 79-91; and lay social theories, 27-37; political representations and problem solving of, 16-23; political thinking of, 54-55; political tolerance of, 40-50; reasoning of, 55-62
Ajzen, I., 55, 62
Atkin, C., 80, 91
Authority, institutional, and children, 68-77
Avery, P. G., 8, 39, 40, 41, 50, 51

Baddeley, J., 30, 38
Beck, I., 13, 23, 24
Beliefs: children's, about organizational roles, 70-76; establishment of, 27; instrumental, 54, 55; social construction of, 69-70; social-ecological study of, 95-105; symbolic, 54, 55-56
Bell, C., 97, 105
Berti, A. E., 14, 24, 66, 77
Billig, M., 28, 30, 38
Bingham, R. D., 44, 50
Bombi, A. S., 14, 24, 66, 77
Bronfenbrenner, U., 9, 10, 95-96, 98, 104, 105
Brookes, M., 80, 92
Buckalew, L. W., 54, 62
Bureaucracies: and children's beliefs, 70-76; and cognitive development, 66-70; and socialization, 65-66
Bureaucratization, 65

Carey, S., 7, 10
Chi, M.T.H., 15, 24
Chicanos, study of social order socialization of, 80-91
Children: and authority, 68-69, 76-77; organizational roles beliefs of, 70-76
Citizenship, education for, 3-4

Coffield, K. E., 54, 62
Cognitive development: and authority, 66-69; and beliefs, 27; and process of development, 69-70
Cognitive psychology, and political socialization framework, 12-16
Colby, A., 29, 38
Cook, T. E., 89, 91
Corbett, M., 45, 50
Cullen, J. L., 71, 77

Damon, W., 68, 69, 77
Dennis, J., 40, 41, 50, 79, 91
Development. See Cognitive development
Dickinson, J., 69, 73, 77
Dissent. See Political tolerance
Dreeban, R., 71, 77
Duveen, G., 12, 24

Easton, D., 79, 91
Ecological transitions, 96
Emler, N., 9, 65, 66, 69, 71, 73, 77
Environmental movement, 5
Erikson, E. H., 40, 50
Events. See World events
Exosystem, 96

Family, and social order socialization, 85-86
Feather, N. T., 30, 38
Fishbein, M., 55, 62
Fiske, S., 12, 15, 24
French, P., 97, 105, 106
Furnham, A., 30, 38
Furth, H., 68, 69, 77

Gainsburg, J., 57, 63
Garcia, F. C., 79, 91
Gibson, J. L., 44, 46, 50
Gilligan, C., 30, 35, 38
Glaser, J. M., 50
Graber, D. A., 13, 24
Green, D. P., 50
Greenberg, E., 79, 91
Greenstein, F. I., 79, 91
Gustafsson, G., 80, 92

107

ORDERING INFORMATION

NEW DIRECTIONS FOR CHILD DEVELOPMENT is a series of paperback books that presents the latest research findings on all aspects of children's psychological development, including their cognitive, social, moral, and emotional growth. Books in the series are published quarterly in Fall, Winter, Spring, and Summer and are available for purchase by subscription as well as by single copy.

SUBSCRIPTIONS for 1992 cost $52.00 for individuals (a savings of 20 percent over single-copy prices) and $70.00 for institutions, agencies, and libraries. Please do not send institutional checks for personal subscriptions. Standing orders are accepted.

SINGLE COPIES cost $17.95 when payment accompanies order. (California, New Jersey, New York, and Washington, D.C., residents please include appropriate sales tax.) Billed orders will be charged postage and handling.

DISCOUNTS FOR QUANTITY ORDERS are available. Please write to the address below for information.

ALL ORDERS must include either the name of an individual or an official purchase order number. Please submit your order as follows:
   Subscriptions: specify series and year subscription is to begin
   Single copies: include individual title code (such as CD1)

MAIL ALL ORDERS TO:
   Jossey-Bass Publishers
   350 Sansome Street
   San Francisco, California 94104

FOR SALES OUTSIDE OF THE UNITED STATES CONTACT:
   Maxwell Macmillan International Publishing Group
   866 Third Avenue
   New York, New York 10022

OTHER TITLES AVAILABLE IN THE
NEW DIRECTIONS FOR CHILD DEVELOPMENT SERIES
William Damon, Editor-in-Chief